Messages from the Spirit World
Awakening to your Soul

David Armstrong

Little Swan Publishing 2025

Minnesota

LITTLE SWAN PUBLISHING, JUNE 2025

Copyright © 2014 by David Armstrong

All rights reserved. Published in the United States by Little Swan Publishing, Minnesota.

First Edition January 2014

Second Edition May 2014

Third Edition June 2025 – 978-0-9883750-0-0

Address all inquiries to

David Armstrong

littleswanpublishing@gmail.com

davidarmstrongonline.com

Dedication

I dedicate this book to my partner Meg Edmonson, who stood by me in tough times. She was incredibly helpful, encouraging me to release this information to the world.

Wherever Meg goes, she is a great inspiration and muse to people. She has been my healing partner and business manager since we started our journey together.

Acknowledgements

I would like to first thank Tarver Nova and Paul Edmonson for their many hours of editing and structuring for this book. The spirit world was generous to provide me with their assistance and understandings. I would also like to thank Meg Edmonson for her clever quotes, encouragement on this project and in my life. Special thanks go out to Lisa Ulshafer, who has been my friend, photographer and given me help with professional promotional tools. I also thank my son Benjamin, who has encouraged me to create this book and some of its graphic designs. Benjamin was especially supportive when I first began writing this book.

I would also like to thank my first spiritual trainer Si Wigness, who recognized the abilities in me at a young age. Si has in a sense passed on the torch to me giving me extremely helpful information that made me realize that I had the gift of healing and insight.

Contents

Introduction..1
    My Spirit Guides and Me 3
    A Family with All the Answers..3
    An Education on the Spirit World..4
    Discovering My Healing Ability 6
    Receiving Spiritual Guidance...7
Part I – The Structure of Our Universe...................................11
    Chapter 1 – The Master and Universal Creators....................13
    Chapter 2 – The Universe 17
        Akashic Records...20
    Chapter 3 – The Soul and its Spirits 23
        The Soul's Demands...27
        The Soul's Purpose...27
        One Soul, Many Spirits 29
        The Relationship Between Souls 30
        Karma 30
        The Afterlife 31
    Chapter 4 – Your Spirit's Functions 33
        Nourishing Your Spirit, Finding Your Purpose..................35
        The Malnourished Spirit...37
        The Malnourished Spirit in Practice 40
        A Liberated Spirit 41
    Chapter 5 – The Celestial Realm 43
        My Brush with the Afterlife 45
        Sixth Dimension I - Principium..45
        Sixth Dimension II - Proximus...46
        Sixth Dimension III - Medius...46
        Sixth Dimension IV - Quartus..48
        Sixth Dimension V - Eduction...51
        Sixth Dimension VI - Provectus...52
        Sixth Dimension VII - Absolutus 53
        The Seven Levels in Review 53
    Chapter 6 - The Angelic Realm 55
        Resident Angels..56
        Guardian Angels 57
        Archangels 57
        Other Angelics..58
    Chapter 7 - The Macroscopic Realm 61

The Tenth Dimension 61
The Eleventh Dimension 65
The Twelfth Dimension 66
Chapter 8 – The Microscopic Realm 67
Chapter 9 – The Circle of Life 69
Chapter 10 – Science and Spirituality 75
Part 2 – The Structure of the Mind 81
Chapter 11 – Thought Energy 83
Chapter 12 – The Human Mind and Brain 87
Chapter 13 – The Three Minds 91
Chapter 14 – The Conscious Mind 93
   Conscious State I - Suneidesis 93
   Conscious State II – Samone 95
   Conscious State III – Noetic 96
   Conscious State IV – Delusional 97
   Conscious State V – Delirium 99
   Conscious State VI – Comatose 99
   Conscious State VII – Afterlife 100
   An Overview 101
Chapter 15 – The 31 Senses 103
Chapter 16 – The Superconscious Mind 127
   Praying to Your Superconscious Mind 129
   Removing Discordant Programs 135
   The Indirect Prayer 138
   Ego, Super-Ego, and Illogism 138
Chapter 17 – The Subconscious Mind 141
   Clearing Your Subconscious 143
   The Subconscious/Superconscious Relationship 145
   Negative Trapped Emotions 145
   Positive Affirmations 146
Chapter 18 – Above the Three Minds 149
   Conscious Interface 149
   The Universal Mind 152
   Spiritual Access of the Universal Mind 153
Part 3 – Spiritual Communication 157
Chapter 19 – Spirit Communication 159
   Imagination 164
   Pineal Gland 167
   Hypnotism 171

Chapter 20 – Connecting with Your Guides 173
    Guides vs. Angels 177
    Striving to be a Light Worker 180
Chapter 21 – Improving Your Intuition 183
    The Seven Intuitive Senses 183
Chapter 22 – Other Spiritual Beings 189
    Ghouls and Poltergeists 190
Chapter 23 – Short Answers to Controversial Questions 193
Chapter 24 – A Review 195
Conclusion 203

Introduction

The Universe is not what you think it is, and most books available today on spirituality are leading you away from the truth. It took an after-life experience for me to realize this.

Perhaps you've had the feeling that your life has little meaning. But here's the truth: most everyone—no matter how successful they may appear to be—wonders what their true purpose is. What is my role? Where should I live? What job should I take? What is going to make me the happiest person I can be? When am I going to meet my life partner?

I know what you are going through because I had those same questions before I had my after-life experience. It took an enormous wake up call for me to get onto the path that I chose before I was born. Wait you might ask, "Did I hear you right?" The first *'aha'* moment in my life that was transformational for me was my afrer-life experience. I discovered that you all choose a role before you are born and if you feel lost it is just because you are off the intended life path.

In this book, you will learn the answers to many questions about the functions of the Universe and discover yourself through a transformational learning process. You will be able to find happiness and cope with the curve balls that life sends your way. I will teach that the truth leads you toward the satisfaction of the spirit.

There is a huge difference between an after-life experience and a near-death experience. In an after-life your spirit will disconnect from the physical body whereas in a near death experience your spirit is still connected to the flesh. In the afterlife your spirit will leave the third dimension and go back to where your soul resides in what we call the sixth dimension.

I understand that many of you might be wondering if each one of us has the same truth. You might think that your truth is drastically different than another person's truth. And believe me I get that but there is only one truth. We all have a difference of perspective, and ideologies vary from person to person. Entire wars have been fought over a difference of perspective but here is the good news. The truth is always the truth. Hearing truth feels so much better than hearing a lie.

In a sense, I want to be a teacher to lead you toward the truth. This book is about bringing to a realization of the way the Universe operates, how the mind works and what we can do to stay on our intended path. When I was younger, I thought everyone was of love. Truth is the pathway to love. The further you move away from the truth, the more isolated, lonely and depressed you become. I want to change that. I want to teach everyone who is willing to hear what the spirit guides taught me.

Spirit guides are of God I learned when I crossed over. Some of us have this knowing as to what the guides are teaching us, but it does not sound like a voice. It is like a deep telepathic understanding.

When I had my afterlife experience, I met the spirit that I now call my father guide. This guide began to enrich my understanding about my existence. It takes a lot to surprise me, but their information blew my mind.

If you are ready to go on a new journey, then I want to be the new tour guide. I've discovered that knowing the truth, helps you gain wisdom, abundance, love and all the things you desire. It is my hope that this book will be the most transformative work you have read to date. I hope to remove all the false distortions of the world. When you are on your spiritual path, you become excited about life every day.

I know that I have turned my life around by being about truth and I try my best to avoid those who do not speak the truth. This book contains information given to me by my spirit guides. It will reintroduce you to knowledge you have always had but have lost due to the distance from your spirit. This information is your birthright and cannot be hidden forever. Some of it may be familiar, some foreign. Some even may remind you of beliefs from other eras, as this information has been throughout the ages, found and lost again. Remember: this information is not my opinion, but rather the truth from my spirit guides. The truth sets you free and when you hear the truth people often say they get goose bumps.

My guides want to inform humanity about the abilities held within each of you that were placed there to allow you divine grace in living. I am now one of the messengers for the spirit world. The reason the book is titled Messages from the Spirit World is because it is the information I was given plus what I learned in the afterlife.

My intention is not for fame or profit, but for this book to be my service piece to the world. It will help you move closer to the truth. I will teach how the dimensions are structured. Once you gain this knowledge, you will no longer be standing in the dark when it comes to our spirit and soul. The closer you move toward the truth, the closer you get to your spirit.

This book will inform you about the truth of your existence. I will explain to readers where your spirit comes from, and how the spiritual world is structured. Once you can see clearly how you connect with the spirit world, and how the spirit world above works, we can easily understand our purposes here. This is no encyclopedia, either; you will learn many tools to affirm and directly build your connection with the spirit world. With a better understanding of how your mind is structured, and the way your mind connects to the spirit realm, you will be able to see how to access your own truth and more of your spiritual abilities. I won't give all the answers, but I will give you tools to develop them yourself.

My Spirit Guides and Me

I was born on a small family farm in North Dakota. I often played by myself and spent a lot of time at my grandparent's home. They were a major part of my upbringing and ahead of their time in their progressive thinking. They encouraged me to speak my truth.

When I was a young boy, I started hearing from my spirit guides (for short, I like to call them my 'guides'). No, I had not gone crazy; it was not the stereotypical 'voices in your head.' Rather, I often would get a strong impression that someone was talking to me. I didn't 'hear' the voices; it was rather a strong inner knowing in the form of communication. I would see the sentences and then understand what the spirit guides were trying to tell me.

When I first started hearing my guides, they spoke to make their presence known. They didn't want to overload me with too much information at too early an age. They allowed me to stay an imaginative kid, and for that, I sincerely thank them. Additionally, they did pop in every so often to protect me. Once, for example, my brother wanted me to go riding with him on his motorcycle. When I was about to get on, I felt a strong sense that my guides were saying: *don't get on the motorcycle*. But brotherly peer pressure is strong, and I got on the back of his motorcycle. Only a quarter mile down the gravel road, the motorcycle tipped over. I got all scraped up and it was a painful experience for me as a six-year-old kid. This was the first of many lessons for me: whenever I don't listen to my guides, it always ends badly. You would think by now I could do no wrong, but some of us learn lessons the hard way.

A Family with All the Answers

It was a good thing I could hear my spirit guides when I was a child, as they could give me straight answers that I was not able to get from anyone else. Being a curious child, I was always asking my parents and grandparents about how the world functioned. Yet, their answers never satisfied me so I continued asking irritating questions. My parents had different ideas than my grandparents, so it furthered my confusion. My father was conservative and my mother a bit more liberal. My mother went to church every Sunday while my father went only a few times a year on special occasions. My father claimed he was more of an atheist, whereas my mother and grandmother believed whatever their religious leaders taught them. My grandfather, on the other hand, was more spiritual than religious. My father did believe that we lived on after the body would die but he believed that we all reincarnate. My mother insisted we had only one life to live. Their differences only led me to a stronger degree of confusion.

Of course, I wanted to know more about my spirit guides. At that time, I was still too young to get concrete spiritual answers from my guides; they were simply watching over me.

I remember asking my parents if there were such things as ghosts when I was young. My father said there could be, and my mother said there was no such thing, So I asked my grandfather hoping to find some middle ground or perhaps a consensus. My grandfather told me that ghosts are real, but they couldn't hurt you. I liked that one, so I went with it. I wondered if I was speaking to ghosts, but at any rate, I felt safe that ghosts couldn't hurt me.

I must have kept asking questions about guides, because eventually my mother became concerned that I was hearing voices. She worried those voices could be ghosts even though she told me she didn't believe in them. She taught me to say a prayer that I recited nearly every night before going to bed. "Dear God, please lead me and guide me and protect me from all harm. And God bless momma and papa and brother and sister and grandpa and grandma." I guess I felt I would be 'protected.' Little did she know that my spirit guides and angels were doing the protecting? To this day, I do believe that my diligent prayers did help strengthen my connection to my guides. It kept me aware that there was something more to life than what I could see, and most importantly, that we could ask for protection from the spiritual world. I learned not to be afraid of things I could not see.

An Education on the Spirit World

As I matured, I talked to my mother about my spirit guides, but she became angry with me and told me that guides weren't real. She started punishing me for lying, and I started to feel ashamed of myself. I started relying on my grandparents for information about the Universe, because I thought they might be more objective. I believed that my mother didn't love me, so I looked for ways to gain her favor.

Introduction

Sometimes, my spirit guides made my relationship with my mother more difficult. One day, when I was five years old, my father had baled some hay in the small field near our house. I thought I was being helpful by bringing the bales to the barn by hauling them in my little red wagon. Rather than pull the wagon by hand, I tied it to the riding lawnmower. In my little five-year-old brain, it made perfect sense that a riding lawnmower and wagon could be the easiest way to get the bales to the barn.

In the first trip, I had loaded only one bale on the wagon. It was too heavy to lift by the guides were kind enough to help me by the process of levitation. With the guides' help, the bales floated effortlessly onto the wagon. I did not even need to lay a hand on them, so we stacked two. On the next trip, I thought it would be more efficient to stack three bales at a time, so I remember commanding the bales to get onto the wagon but the guides did this for me. At the time, I was not sure how this worked but I had no reason to believe that this was abnormal.

As I passed the house, my mother saw me go by with a wagon stacked with three bales. She spotted me through her kitchen window when washing dishes. She must have thought I could use some help lifting them off, so she ran outside to help me. My mother noticed when she lifted the first bale that they were too heavy for such a young boy to lift. I remember her asking me, "How on Earth did you lift these all the way up there. When I told her that, I just told them to get onto the wagon, my mother got quite angry. She thought I was lying to her and, again, she punished me. She told me to go to my room and she took away all my toys, which at that age, was severe punishment. I didn't ask my guides to help me again until I was much older.

I knew in my heart that I did not lie to her but could not explain in words my world. Not only that, but I was also getting tired of being scolded for no reason so I vowed never to do that again.

The guides left me without communication during my formative years, and for a while, I really thought that my parents and grandparents had the answers to the way life was meant to be. I started to believe that there was a heaven and hell. However, even during this time, I also believed that my father and grandfather were encouraging me to follow my guides and my personal spiritual compass. They encouraged me to listen to my intuition. As I grew older, I did listen, but I did not always follow my spirit guides suggestions. My grandfather used to call intuition business acumen and he felt more comfortable with that term

Discovering My Healing Ability

By the time I was about ten years old, a psychic healer named Si Wigness who encouraged me to tune in to my guides. Si recognized that I could also heal, and he asked me to help him heal a man that was dying from cancer. Medical doctors had tried everything, but it seemed hopeless for this man. The doctors suggested he return home to make his final arrangements. He purportedly had only two weeks left to live. Si asked my dad to bring me over to see if I could heal him.

At this time, I was unaware of just how powerful healing abilities were, but Si told me to just to follow my guides instructions. After fifteen minutes of holding the man's wrist while my guides worked through me, they said to tell the person to drink juiced carrots for the next thirty days. He said had nothing to lose and decided to try it. After many weeks, he was feeling much better and returned to his doctor for a checkup. There were no signs of cancer, and they were baffled. He ended up living for another twenty-two years.

After seeing this person healed from his cancer, my father now believed in my ability to heal others. My mother was another matter, and it took many years to convince her that there was anything to it. I later understood that part of the reason she had been so resistant was that she wanted me to have a 'normal' upbringing. She was afraid that I may be ridiculed by my peers.

Over time, I learned that I wasn't the only one with spiritual abilities. When I was still a child, my grandfather showed me how to witch for water. *Witching* for water is a country term for dowsing. It's a process of holding two pieces of firm copper wire or sticks out in front of you while you walk around a property until the rods or sticks cross each other. The location on the property where they cross reveals where you will find a source of water for a well. At my age, I thought this was completely normal. It seemed funny that grandpa did it for others; why would he need to help others find water. Could they not do this for themselves? It wasn't until I was about fourteen when I saw that my brother was unable to witch for water so I realized my grandfather had a special ability.

When I was a teenager, my grandfather showed me how powerful he was as a healer, but it was not something that he ever talked about with others. I had stepped on a rusty nail on our farm while tearing down an old building. Over the next few days, my foot began to swell and hurt. Four days later, it had grown to twice its normal size. My grandfather took me to see a doctor. I only expected to get a shot, but the doctor was certain that my foot should be amputated. I remember well my grandfather's words, "You're not taking my grandson's foot!" Although he did not tell me at the time, that he knew what he needed to do.

Over the next week or more, he bathed my foot in Epsom salt and warm water, and continually applied massage. He did that about five or six times a day. By the end of the week, the swelling had reduced dramatically and some of the redness was gone. Eventually my foot returned to its normal size. This proved to me that my grandfather too was a healer, and I surmised that these abilities must run in the family.

Receiving Spiritual Guidance

In my life, I have received enormous amounts of information from my guides. I want to share as much of this information that I can, and I will try to focus on things that will be easy to understand

Remember, in my prayer as a child, I had asked my spirit guides to lead me, to guide me, and to keep me from harm. Understand that I continually put myself in harm's way, but I am not even sure why it happened so many times. Even as an adult, I was gravitating toward danger, so I made myself a promise to start listening to my spirit guides better ad follow their suggestions wherever possible.

Once when I was going into town to unload a car off a dolly, the spirit guides suggested that I go home immediately. I thought to myself, no, I have work to do! I will just go and unload this car off the dolly at the repair shop, and then go home to have breakfast. The guides practically screamed at me to return home, but I wouldn't listen. When I got to the repair shop, I noticed something funny about how the straps on the dolly were attached, but before I could do anything, it came loose. I couldn't react quickly enough, so my first thought was to hold the car from rolling off the dolly to prevent it from slamming into the truck behind me. I should have called out to my spirit guides for help; I'm sure they would have assisted, but it was too late. I got my arm smashed between the vehicles. My arm was nearly severed, and the pain was unbearable. I drove myself home and my wife drove me to the nearest hospital, where an excellent appendage reattachment specialist just happened to have traveled there as well. He was able to save my arm. I was lucky and blessed, the spirit world had orchestrated for this specialist to be there for me. It was an extremely hard lesson to learn. It looked as though once again I was learning my lessons the hard way. I hope that I will never be so bullheaded when it comes to listening to my guides again.

Many people have been hearing from guides for thousands of years including some famous individuals. Albert Einstein was one of those lucky people that guides were working with every day. He was a famous scientist that taught us many esoteric ideas. These ideas were notions not considered or at least not written about in the academic world. He set out to prove scientifically that his notions were correct. His theories were ahead of the times, and he created a paradigm shift in the way people viewed science. I asked myself the question: was Albert Einstein just having foggy notions, or was he getting messages from the spirit world just as I was? My guides explained that Albert Einstein spent every waking day of his life talking to a multitude of guides. He had asked to play this role before he even incarnated. Now his theories are taught in schools throughout the world. He seemed to understand things about the Universe that others did not. I liked his notion that the Universe is not what we think it is. Einstein, for the most part, believed that the Universe could react to our desires.

I have noticed that most people have rigid belief systems. I know that some people that have had good intentions had ended up teaching mistruths. Following a rigid belief system does not allow new information to be added and will not provide you with a rich, fulfilled life. I find that if you follow your inner sense of truth, you will most likely live a happy life, even if it differs from your cultural teachings.

I would like to share with everyone some teachings from my guides that helped me with my life. I also want to make it as simple as I can so that no one feels lost or alienated. This is not meant to be a book that will bore you to tears, but to be a light, easy read with a few new terms thrown in. I plan to write a more advanced book, but this one geared toward educating people about the truth of the Universe and how this truth can directly help us in our daily lives. This is not a daily living guide to remind us of our bad habits. However, it will have some practical information about things you can do to improve your life and quite a lot about the physical realm that you live in.

The Earth is a vast place, and you are currently on tour here. For some people it is a short tour and for others it can last much longer. You have the free will to choose what you want to do with your life. If you waste your lives doing meaningless things that don't inspire you then you have no one to blame but yourself. If you look for a scapegoat for your misgivings, you will not have learned any lessons. There are no misgivings, only opportunities to gain wisdom and understanding about the human condition and the way the Universe works. If you try to blame things on others, you are hurting our chance to live an enriched life. Your success depends directly on how much you are willing to grow spiritually and learn. I hope that this book will inspire you to get out of any ruts you are in so that you can experience a more inspired life.

If any part of this book hits a chord, please remember to share it with others. However, remember that not everyone is ready to receive this information, and no one likes to be hit over the head with it. Just remember this as you are reading the book. Humanity needs to step out of the dark and into the light. These messages were sent though David in order that the truth is known. If you are stepping out into the light, you will be energetically much more attractive to others around you. Remember you came to Earth to think and not to let others show you how to think.

The fact that a person is reading this book is no accident. It is meant to inspire people who want to make positive changes in the world. Even making a change in your own consciousness creates a ripple effect in the human mass consciousness, which in turn, affects all of humanity. Together, we can make a difference in humanity, so there is much to learn.

Part I – The Structure of Our Universe

In this section, I will talk about the general structure of the Universe and spiritual world, and how you are connected to it. I will explain what you were created for and how your soul and spirit (yes, you have both) work. In Part II, you will learn how the mind functions, as well as its many hidden abilities. Once you understand the fundamentals of the Universe, of *you*, you will be better able to tap into those abilities. In Part III, I will further explain about how you interact with the spirit world, and how you can improve this connection.

The good news is this: we can all tap into the spirit world to learn the spiritual truth. We are searching for the truth, and we know that the truth will set us free. It is time to awaken.

Chapter 1 – The Master and Universal Creators

You and everything you know has come from a universal energy that just is and always has been. The spirit world calls this universal energy the Master Creator.

A simple definition: the Master Creator is an all-encompassing energy to which we are all connected. Most dimensions are overlapping one another but the Master Creator is in a dimension that is far away from Earth. The Master Creator is difficult to describe by the words of the English language. Some people call the Master Creator "God," while some people call it, "The Creator" or "The Source", and some people simply see it as the energy that binds us all. The terminology varies greatly in different religions. For the purposes of this book, we will use the term Master Creator.

The Master Creator has created everything and is always learning about its own creation. The Master Creator connects to everything in existence, including our souls, and it integrates all that we do and experience. Our soul stores all of the information we have ever experienced in each lifetime and passes on our experiences to the Master Creator. There is no need to worry that all of this information will clog your soul; it is so vast that it will never run out of memory.

We must understand that the Master Creator is so vast, so encompassing, that it does not create us directly. Rather, the Master Creator made entities called Universal Creators. There is one Universal Creator for each Universe in existence. If the Master Creator wants to create a new Universe, then it creates a new Universal Creator. When a Universal Creator wants to create a new galaxy, it uses the information from all the souls that are in its Universe. It can then create a more diverse galaxy with the information it has gathered.

When I first learned about the Master Creator, of course I wanted to know what created the Master Creator. My spirit guides' answer was quite shocking to me. They said, "Nothing times nothing created a spark." The spark was a thought. I asked myself, "How could it be *thought*, just pure thought?" This confused me at first. It was hard for me—as it probably is for anyone on Earth—to break out of 3rd-dimensional perceptions. Nevertheless, it is true. All of existence started with a single thought.

Master Creator
Universal Creator
Soul
Spirit
Physical Body

Later, you may get a better handle on understanding existence and the concept of infinity when we discuss how all of the dimensions in our Universe are created to work together in an endless, circular fashion. This circular cycle is apparent all throughout our Universe. The Universe was created by thought, and all thoughts are energies with special properties. I am not here to tell you what those special properties are, because even the spirit world says they're difficult to understand. There are no words in our languages to describe such things as these special properties, the Master

Chapter 1 – The Master and Universal Creators

Creator, or the Universal Creator, just like there are no words that can adequately describe love.

Chapter 2 – The Universe

The Universe is a living organism created by the Universal Creator. It consists of five realms, which include thirteen dimensions. We are not able to perceive all thirteen dimensions because higher dimensions vibrate at rates faster than our physical senses can perceive. They can only be experienced through our psychic senses. In general, lower dimensions do not fully perceive the higher dimensions if at all.

The 13th dimension is named the microscopic realm and does not have any life forms but consists of the energetic building blocks of the Universe. This includes the tiniest aspects of our Universe, things like atoms, molecules and various types of energy units. Spirits are not sent to the 13th dimension since it is just the building blocks.

The experience of the other twelve dimensions is known as the Circle of Life, or the Evolutionary Cycle. Note this model is simplified for humans to understand.

First, let's start with the realm that you live in. The 1st, 2nd and 3rd dimensions are part of the physical realm. Quantum physics goes into detail on the definition of dimensions and can be quite complicated. Therefore, to keep it simple, I will explain what roughly exists in each dimension and not delve into any physics. The 1st dimension includes things like rocks, minerals, and microbial life forms. The 2nd dimension includes things such as plants and insects. The 3rd dimension includes humans, mammals, birds, reptiles, fish, or complex life forms found on other planets.

The 4th, 5th, and 6th dimensions are each part of the celestial realm. You enter the celestial realm frequently in the dream state and in between incarnations. Note ghosts are people who have died and are stuck between the 3rd and 4th dimension. Eventually, either their spirit guide or guardian angel will convince them to go through the white tunnel that leads from the 4th dimension to the 6th. The 4th dimension includes disembodied spirits like goblins, demons and nicer entities like fairies, leprechauns, and nature spirits. The 5th dimension includes light beings who live in astral form on astral planets. The astral body is like a light body that is all energetic. We cannot see them or their planets because they vibrate at a much higher frequency. The 6th dimension is where all the souls in the Universe eternally reside. It is often referred to as Heaven. The 6th dimension has seven levels which will be described in more detail later in this book.

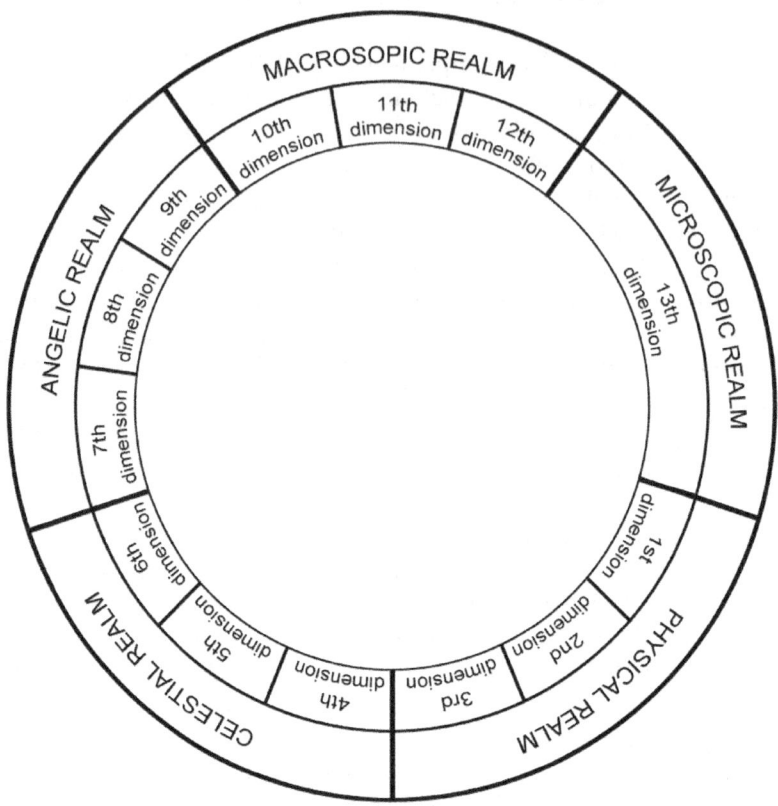

The 7th, 8th, and 9th dimensions are all part of the Angelic Realm. Angels and other advanced beings reside in this realm. The 7th dimension consists of the resident angels. There are trillions of them, and they go out into the Universe to create or restore harmony. They have thousands of different departments. Each department is assigned a different task like steering animals away from natural disasters, healing infants in utero, helping to connect people in love or business relationships, etc. The 8th dimension consists of the guardian angels whose tasks are to help spirits return to their soul at the end of their life experience or intervene in a disaster when it is not their time to die, plus they work on planetary harmony. The 9th dimension consists of archangels who work at the universal level to create or restore harmony. Archangels give direction to the guardian angels and the guardian angels direct the resident angels. There are other advanced benevolent beings that live in the angelic realm too. Some of them aid humanity and some have tasks elsewhere.

The 10th, 11th, and 12th dimensions are the macroscopic realm also known as the creator realm. The 10th dimension is the universal library where all knowledge and experiences are stored. The 11th & 12th dimension creator committees use the library as a resource for their creations. It is also a place where councils aid advanced spirits in choosing their next life incarnation. The 10th dimensional library is also used by spirits to experience different types of existences. For example, if they want to experience being an eagle or what existence is like on another planet before they incarnate there. Spirits can only experience what has happened previously. They need to incarnate to experience their own personal desires. The 11th dimension is where co-creators work with the Universal Creator to create what goes on planets. For example, monkeys, broccoli, humans, etc. The 12th dimension is where co-creators work with the Universal Creator to create planets, solar systems, and galaxies.

There is no one dimension more important than the other. Spirits experience all dimensions to complete the twelve-dimensional Evolutionary Cycle. Our soul always resides in the 6th dimension. For the soul to experience the other dimensions, it send a tiny spark of itself, called the spirit, out to experience another dimension. Nothing has a beginning or an end in this dimensional model. After completing each of the twelve dimensions, a soul can choose to begin again by entering any dimension it wishes. Each time a spirit travels through the twelve dimensions, its transit of those dimensions becomes easier. Spirits continue to move through the Evolutionary Cycle because there are always more places and things to experience. Remember, Universal Creator is developing new galaxies all the time.

The number of incarnations that each soul has varies greatly. Some souls have lived dozens of lives in the Physical Realm and may have lived thousands of lives in the Macroscopic Realm beforehand. It isn't unusual for a soul to have experienced more than a hundred-thousand lives. You can never comprehend adequately just how old the Universe is. It may suffice to say that the Universe is infinitely old. I was told that our solar system is one of the youngest in this Universe.

Even though, the sheer scale of the Universe is overwhelming, know that as a member of this Universe, you have eternity to explore all that exists. Often during sleep, we move beyond our conscious limitations and experience other dimensions. In the dream state, your spirit can move out of the physical body and travel. This is called astral travel, which refers to the concept of the spirit briefly moving out of the physical body into another realm or dimension while keeping an electrical connection to it. This occurs naturally every time you sleep, but rarely do you remember it. You might recall some of these experiences as dreams. People recall that they were flying in their dreams, which could be a good example of your spirit doing astral traveling. A spirit can astral travel to other cities, continents, or even planets in a short time. You may not remember or record the experience consciously, but your soul records everything. Astral travel is an easy way to experience the other dimensions but only if you have conscious recall.

I've had only one conscious astral travel experience myself. I was in college at the time. As I was leaving my body, the sounds of the Universe were deafening. It was closest to the ruckus a freight train will make as it rolls down the track, though I had never heard an Earthly sound quite like it. There are spirits in the next dimension, numerous as a crowded New York subway. It spooked me, so in an instant I jumped back into my body and have not attempted this again. During astral travel, you get a vague sense of how complex the Universal Creator has made the dimensions.

Akashic Records

The Universe's knowledge is stored away in something called the Akashic records. The Akashic records are like a vast storehouse, sometimes referred to as the Akashic records. [The spirit world refers to an entity they call Akashi, who was the one who conceived of the idea to keep all of our lifetimes recorded.] The Akashic records all the events that have occurred within our Universe in all the dimensions. Earth's history is in its own separate location in the Akashic records, and within that location are separate places for each species on Earth. Humanity has its own file, which is referred to as the human mass consciousness. All the things that each spirit experiences are automatically fed into its own Akashic record file through a process involving a permanent connection to the soul.

Possibilities of future events are held in another structure, not the Akashic records.

You may be surprised to learn that you can access these records. After all, they are yours. However, you must have love and positive intent to access our personal Akashic records.

Why would anyone want to open his or her own records? It could be to discover their purpose in life. It could be to strengthen their spirit. Alternatively, it could be done out of curiosity. The spirit world does not

Chapter 2 – The Universe

think it is a good idea to open your own Akashic records if you are just curious about our previous lives. Rather, you should focus on your current life and not allow your past to interfere with your purpose.

You are the protector of your own Akashic records. If it is not in your best interest for another person to peer into your Akashic records, then any request made by that person will be refused. Another person must not tempt you to allow them access to your records. This is private, proprietary information that is much like a safety deposit box in a bank.

In the Akashic library, there is information that is not proprietary. This information may be your collective experiences, your mutual understandings. It is your shared life. You may receive these impressions from the Akashic records without accessing the Akashic library directly. Your soul will send you the information it deems to be helpful. These impressions may be the collective experiences of another individual. There is no record as to whom these experiences belong, and for all you know, the experiences could be part of your own past lifetimes.

Many things may not be pertinent for spirits to know when they incarnate on Earth. That information could contaminate experiences, instead of being beneficial. The spirit world will rarely give exact information, such as the day the body will die. This would be entirely unsuitable, as revealing the precise details of future events.

You will not be sent information that could affect large segments of the population in an unproductive fashion. For your own karmic protection, the spirit world does not want you to send advice to others based on the probability of a catastrophic future event. Because there are so many possible outcomes, my guides do not communicate to me too much prophetic information. The future is not set, and timelines are constantly shifting and multiplying.

Although you may not want to access your Akashic records, it's still good to know that these records exist. Knowing these records exist allow you to feel less alone and lost in your life. Your experiences are not simply momentary whims, but rather are records important to the Universe. The spirit is remembering and cherishing everything you do. In addition, some day, you may be allowed to relive your memories again through those Akashic records.

Chapter 3 – The Soul and its Spirits

What is the soul, and how is it different from the spirit? I've found that almost no one can agree upon what a soul is, and some believe that the soul and the spirit are the same thing. However, religions do not teach anything that is close to the truth.

My mother had once said that we all have a soul, and that it lives on for an eternity. This is true, but as a young boy, I could not convince my mother that I was hearing from guides, and they'd given me a higher understanding than she had.

The information in this book does not come from anything I have read in other books on the same subject. In fact, I have found little out there on the subject, and when I did some research many years ago, I found information that the guides did not agree with. So here is the truth.

Although it is difficult, we can nail down a rough definition of the soul. The spirit world defines the *soul* as a spark of consciousness that is immortal. The soul is the direct result of a *transpirational* thought of a Universal Creator. A transpirational thought means a thought that has no ending. It just goes out into the Universe indefinitely.

The soul then sends out a spark of its own energy, called a spirit, into the Universe to experience a lifetime. The spirit world defines the *spirit* as a spark of consciousness from the soul that undergoes transformation. This soul is so much larger than the spirit that it would be difficult to comprehend just how vast its energy is. It may send a spirit to Earth or another planet in the Universe. A spirit can also be sent into other dimensional realities to experience a life, but usually the soul sticks with the dimension it is trying to master.

Because you are only a small portion of your soul, being little more than a tiny spark of it, you may have forgotten all your previous incarnations. It is easy, then, to understand why you are so diverse in your thinking. How could any of us agree when we are such small parts of the whole? Our spirit itself only carries a small aspect of our souls understanding.

There are many aspects to a soul, but it is hard to explain due to lack of vocabulary to describe the sheer complexity of the soul. Back when societies spoke Latin more commonly, there was a deeper vocabulary for understanding the spiritual nature. Latin had more than a thousand words to explain various components of the soul and its experience. In fact, the term *psychology* means, in Latin, 'the study of the soul.'

You will begin by breaking down a common misunderstanding. Many think that *soul* is a synonym for *spirit*. However, according to my spirit guides, there is a vast difference. Remember, the soul is a spark of the creator, and the spirit is a spark of the soul. A spirit is only a tiny spark of consciousness from the soul. Your soul resides in the celestial realm, and it stays there while you live your physical life. Your spirit comes from the Celestial Realm and enters the physical realm; your spirit is what occupies the body when you are alive. When you die, your spirit returns to the Celestial Realm, where it connects to your soul. As you can see, spirit is cut from the same cloth as the soul but is a much smaller piece. The soul is so immense it is nearly impossible to comprehend. As the spirit is to the soul, so is the soul made up of the same energy as the Universal Creator, just a much smaller unit.

The reason the spirit world chooses the word *spirit* is because the word means the breath of life. A body without the "breath of life" is just a conglomeration of atoms. The spirit starts the body's breathing and all its automated functions. So, you are getting a little closer now to showing that the spirit's function is the most important to life. The spirit is limitless, held by no boundaries. It does not have a physical shape. The spirit is the unlimited essence that breathes life into the physical body and passes all knowledge to the Celestial Realm. If you understand only this, you have accomplished something great today.

Upon death, it is necessary for your spirit to return to the soul so it can be recharged. You might wonder whether the soul sends out the same spark in the next incarnation or whether your same consciousness goes back out into a new life. The soul will eventually send out the same spark, but it will have a new agenda and usually is veiled from knowing it's previous lives. Not only that, but your soul can also send out many spirits at once, so technically, your soul may very well be living many, many lives right now.

Although you are only one tiny piece of your soul, do not let yourself feel small. The development of the soul depends entirely on the work of the spirits. In other words, your soul is really counting on you, one of its spirits. Your mission is unspeakably important, whether you understand it or not. Most broadly, your mission is simple: it is to bring joy, expression, and meaning to the Creator. Both the soul and its spirits are working toward that purpose. Each spirit is deepening the soul's awareness, learning values, and bringing a greater wholeness to your soul.

Your soul's primary purpose is to translate experiences back to the Universal Creator, which passes the experiences on to the Master Creator.

Chapter 3 – The Soul and its Spirits

You are always observing and collecting information from your time in the Universe. The Universal Creator gathers this information so that it can create better Universes. Your life experiences influence how the Universal Creator makes new worlds. In addition, your experiences are stored in the Universal library for others to learn from. Think about this the next time you feel unworthy or small.

The soul is interested in storing wisdom, and the spirit is the vessel that brings the wisdom to the soul. It does so through what the spirit world calls the superconscious highway. This superconscious highway is an energetic pathway that is sometimes referred to as the "silver chord" because of its energetic properties. The superconscious highway is not an extension of the spirit but is just a pathway that connects you directly to your soul. This "silver chord" is only disconnected once your spirit returns to your soul in the 6th dimension.

All your experiences are recorded by the soul but may not be so important for the spirit to remember. Here is an example: let us say you walk by an apple tree. Consciously, you may have noticed that there are apples on the trees. Your soul can record that association. It can even go as far as understanding exactly how many apples are on that tree. Your conscious mind is unaware of how many apples are on the tree, but your spiritual mind tracks exact details and sends it on to your soul.

There are people gifted at retrieving information stored in the soul. In the movie "Rain Man," this gifted individual appears to be different than we are in many ways. In one of the scenes, a box of toothpicks is spilled, and he instantly knows how many are on the floor. He is simply connected to the soul better than we are and retrieves that information in a second. Remember, this movie is based on a real person. This is a good example of just how much information the soul can store. A part of your mind decides whether this information is going to be helpful to your current spiritual existence. If it is not that important, it will not store this information. The spiritual mind then acts like a filter, but the spirits experiences are always recorded by the soul.

Your spirit manages knowledge differently than your soul. Your spirit collects knowledge and then transmits it to your soul. Your soul adds it to the soul's previously stored knowledge to create wisdom. Your spirit keeps all the information from your present life and the soul keeps information from all your lives. To distinguish the difference: knowledge is the superficial data we learn from day to day, such as where you left our keys, and where you live. Wisdom, on the other hand, is more fundamental: knowing right from wrong, and understanding the world as it is. Wisdom is a collection of data that builds a basis of understanding. Your soul stores all the knowledge you acquire, and the subconscious mind stores the knowledge deemed appropriate by your superconscious mind. The subconscious mind does not keep wisdom. I will discuss this function of the superconscious mind later.

You've all met people who lack wisdom. They are not simply forgetful or ignorant, that's a lack of knowledge. Instead, they are people who steal, lie, and don't seem to be considerate of others. They are selfish and greedy. These people lack wisdom. You'll often find these people in positions of power, or in the prison system due to their self-centered nature. They're not stupid. They're simply power-hungry, and disregard those around them.

The mere fact that you have been created to help the Universal Creator does not make you subservient in any way. The soul has its own interests and agenda, and it comes with a complexity of purposes. It's the soul's decision as to where to send a spirit. The Universal Creator does not make that determination. The spirit world says that each soul wants to have experiences, to create, to advance to liberation, and to incarnate into different life forms. The soul experiences all these things through the spirit. The reason it wants to do these things varies from soul to soul, but they have many of the same purposes.

I have experienced many different professions, made many different relationships in my life. Can you imagine if the Universal Creator did not allow for such a diverse life experience? Each different profession will lead you to a different category of people and experiences. For example, my time as a farmer was vastly different from my time as a manufacturer. Now my experiences have moved onto healing and the field of paranormal studies. As you would guess, I'm not meeting the same types of people as I did in farming or manufacturing. This greatly develops my spiritual understandings. It is easier to understand what different groups of people are coping with in their lives when you have been one of them. As such, the soul chooses to incarnate on different continents, different planets, and different species. It too wishes to experience and understand diversity. There are heavy demands placed on the spirit by the soul. When you become disconnected from your soul, then you do not understand what these demands are.

Prior to incarnating your spirit makes an agreement with your soul, a *soul contract*, to experience and achieve various things. Maybe it wanted to experience playing the violin or divorce or invent something? Your spirit knows, but our personality becomes heavily veiled once we incarnate and we often struggle to figure out what exactly we are here to achieve. The following are some general aspects our soul wants us to accomplish.

The Soul's Demands

The soul has many expectations for its spirits, but here is a short list of its basic demands. One demand is *fulfillment*; your soul wants you to have a whole, complete experience, with a whole gamut of emotional, physical, and mental activities. It expects *completion*; finishing plans that you had promised yourself for this life, and those from past lives never achieved. It wants *inspiration*; you didn't come here to expand only your own consciousness, but also to inspire your soul group, your soul family, or all of humanity. It demands *imperial justice*; with so much injustice in the world, the soul wants you to do your part to help make things right. You are not expected to do it all, but you can be one cog in the wheel of justice. The soul wants you to be *creative*, expanding on your current level of thinking and coming up with new ways and ideas to assist humanity. Lastly, your soul expects *purification*, of both you and others. Purify your thoughts and help others with theirs. If you direct someone toward fear and doubt, they will go in that direction. If you direct someone towards hope and love, they will go in that direction. A few people can affect more with hope and love than with fear and doubt. Hope and love are a more sustaining combination than fear and doubt, and leads to a stronger spirit with more energy. There are plenty of lesser demands of the soul, but these are the primaries.

The Soul's Purpose

You've now learned about the soul's general agenda. But what of your specific soul's purpose? When I had my near-death experience, I wanted to know what I came here to do and why I was created. My spirit guides first had to explain to me the process of becoming a soul and the process of becoming a spirit, as I have explained in the previous section. What I found is that our souls all have similar purposes. You know that the Universal Creator formed you, but it allows you free will to choose your goals before incarnating. This provides the tools you need to exist. You send a spark of your soul into a physical being to experience, to create, to advanced, to assist others, and to convey to the Universal Creator. This is a platform and how you build on that platform is the decision of the soul.

You might have come to Earth to be a musician, a scientist, or a carpenter and any type of involvement can be a tool to help you achieve your soul's purpose. Perhaps you are coming for artistic expressions to bring greater wholeness and joy to humanity, and this could be only one of the possible soul purposes you are here to experience. At the same time, you may choose to have a family. Having a family is not only an act of assisting others but offers plenty of opportunities for personal growth through family relationships. The soul's purpose is an inner value or need that it wants fulfilled in a lifetime. You came here to work on multiple things but usually have one primary purpose. What you chose for your outer activities will greatly enhance your inner development.

If you are in a profession that is out of line with your soul's purposes, you will feel alienated from the Universal Creator. There is no spiritual satisfaction in doing things that don't accomplish soul growth. My clients say all the time that they feel trapped and need to pay the bills. The Universe does align itself to support you and fulfill your needs when you get on your spiritual path. Perhaps you don't need the lavish things that your current job is providing, especially if those things are not bringing you spiritual satisfaction. If you allow yourself to be stuck in a rut, then the Universe may think that you want more of the same experience and that you have not learned the lesson. You have a choice to get into a desired field of study once you get over your self-imposed limitations. You will then feel your spirit gaining energy, and your life begin to flow with purpose.

Do you strive to be inspired? Inspired is a two-part word. The first part is 'in' and the second part comes from the word 'spirit'. So, when you are inspired, you are in *spirit*. This is as close to your spirit as you can become. When you do inspiring things, you get excited, you change your attitudes, and you may even excel at various things. Being in spirit is the closest you can become to your soul.

When I am performing healings for people, the biggest problem they tell me about is that they complain they aren't doing anything inspiring in their lives. As a result, they experience dissatisfaction and ill health. The spirit world instructs them to make a list all the things they would enjoy doing, and then endeavor to work in those fields that are closest to their spirit. When you can find an activity or job that uses the most attributes of who you are, you will feel a wholeness and satisfaction. You are then using and being more of your full self-daily, and you feel a stronger connection to your spirit and soul.

Here is a strange question that scientists have tried to address. Does a spirit weigh anything? I was surprised to find out that the answer is no, hardly any measurable amount. I wondered how that could be. Experiments have shown that when the body dies and the spirit passes out of the body, as much as 2.2 grams have been lost. Their explanation for this phenomenon makes perfect sense to me. When the spirit enters a physical presence, it starts a vortex of energy circulating in all the cells. This creates magnetism in the body. The magnetism then creates a pull with the Earth's gravitational forces. Then we are all gravitational, I thought, each contributing a tiny bit of your own gravity to Earth.

One Soul, Many Spirits

As I have noted, your soul is vast, it is possible to live many lives at one time. It may be hard to believe this, I know; I first thought this was a stretch. I was surprised to see during my afterlife experience that you have this ability. Sometimes the soul will even send spirits to many planets at the same time. Two people can belong to the same soul. Two or even three incarnates from one soul are common. There are ambitious souls that do many lives at once, but on average, a soul will have only two or three spirits out at a time. For example, I have two others here on Earth who shares my soul. When I first learned this, of course, I was curious who my literal 'soul mates' might be. The spirit guides told me that finding out would be interference with our purposes here.

Of course, you must wonder: why would a soul want to live more than one life at once? It boggles the mind to think that you—that is, that part your soul—could be living not only your life but others' as well. Sometimes, it feels like one life is more than enough. However, you must first understand the sheer scale of your own soul. The soul can expand into other Universes and dimensions. It does not limit itself to incarnations on Earth and is multidimensional. *Multidimensional* means that we are connected to all the dimensions in some way and that you can access all of those dimensions. However, the majority of people are only conscious of the 3rd dimension.

Being a human on Earth has enormous limitations. Most humans are heavily veiled from their soul's greater knowledge. Once you get to the Physical Realm, you don't remember much of what your spiritual nature is and society feeds us distorted, limiting beliefs. You therefore usually do not live up to your full potential. Yet, you need not worry; the Universal Creator does not expect that you will reach your true potential quickly. You may spend thousands of lives learning and growing.

The Relationship Between Souls

A good analogy to describe the relationship between souls is a grape vine. One grape is a soul. A soul is comprised of a multitude of spirits. A cluster of grapes is a soul group. A soul group is a group of spirits that frequently incarnate around each other and play varying support roles. A branch of a grape vine is a soul family. The souls in a soul family are distantly related. The whole grape vine itself is comprised of all the souls in the Universe.

Remember, each species has its own mass consciousness through the Akashic records, which shares understandings between members. For instance, monkeys have their own mass consciousness, as do cats in which they share all their survival skills. Although humans do not appear to be connected to their own species' mass consciousness, they are, and there are many examples of this. For example, the New York Times Sunday crossword puzzle is more difficult in the morning but gets easier as the day goes on. This is because many thousands have worked on it, and their experiences have entered into the human mass consciousness. Another example: you'll notice across history that people tend to come up with the same breakthrough inventions around the same time. For this reason, the patent system evolved. It's a strange phenomenon, to be sure, but what my spirit guides are telling me is true. All are connected to the human mass consciousness, and you can tap into it if you so choose.

Karma

Karma is a Sanskrit word that means action, work or deed. You hear it used all the time as a principle of causality where intent and action of a person will influence the future of that individual. Good deeds will lead to good karma and future happiness while bad deeds will lead to bad karma and unhappiness. Karma got its start in ancient India but is a key concept in many religions such as Hinduism, Buddhism, Jainism, Sikhism, Taoism just to name a few. It is also the act of bringing upon one's own results either in this lifetime or in another. It is the principle of retributive justice that determines a person's state of life and the state of his or her incarnations.

The Master Creator does not hand out karma. That is the responsibility of the soul. Karma is not really a punishment or retribution, but simply an extended expression or consequence of natural acts. Karma is one of the universal laws that states that you bring upon your own destiny from the consequence of your actions.

Karma is an energy that is subtle, and yet pervades the entire Universe. Karma can surround the consciousness of a soul. A soul's karma changes with thoughts as well as actions. Positive actions or thoughts can result in good conditions in one's life, whereas negative actions or thoughts can result in bad conditions. The effects may be seen immediately, or they may be delayed. The delay may even come in a future lifetime. The spirit chooses how and when to work on its own karma.

Good karma can be stored up for a future lifetime. There are those people that just seem to be in a magical flow, and it could mean that they are experiencing the effects of their own positive karma. Perhaps you have met someone who just seems to be in harmony with everything. It would not be a good idea to attempt to control or change people who are already in a magical flow in their lives. That would only build up negative karma for you.

The Afterlife

Upon death, the spirit finds itself looking at the body that it just vacated. With death also comes understanding. Once the physical body is left behind, a completely new body of knowledge will open. It can perceive many things that you couldn't imagine, for now there are no words in the vocabulary to describe them. However, there is a feeling of familiarity, and this feeling is comforting and puts the spirit in a state of ease that it had not experienced since its incarnation. Note that some spirits are not at ease and may not even know that they are dead. They may linger as ghosts for quite some time.

In the afterlife, there are no things of the physical world to confuse you. The truth is pure, and even though you could have experienced the same truth on Earth, you just didn't see it.

Pain is considered a teaching tool on Earth. It can teach you to be more gracious in your dealings with others and to humble you. It is essentially the spirit's lesson to rise above the pain and use the lesson objectively.

Humans can be too focused on the trivialities of life. If they learn to rise above the trivialities and jump out of the emotional cesspool, they can handle the stresses of life with greater ease. Many humans use the stresses of life as an excuse to avoid spiritual needs. It is as if they believe that the spiritual pathway is difficult, but it is the exact opposite. They might not even believe that there is an easier way, so they continue experiencing the pathway of suffering.

In the afterlife, there is no heavy sensation of a body weighing you down. All the things that burdened the body are lifted. The fears that controlled the emotional body no longer exist. The troubles and concerns that consumed everyday thoughts will no longer be plaguing to you. Existing in the afterlife gives clarification to some of the spirit's most difficult questions that were a complete puzzle in your Earthly existence.

Time has no meaning in the afterlife. You can go forward in time or backward in time and view the progression as though you were standing right there. Catastrophic events lose the attachment of fear in the afterlife and the spirit is unaffected.

Humans do create their own destiny, and they all need to understand the concept of unselfish giving. When you give unselfishly, the pathway of destiny that opens is a much different course. Much of the gifts or help that people give to one another come with the expectation that there will be reciprocity. Regardless of your state of health, you should always give the best quality help that you can give without expecting anything in return. In order to excel at giving, you do not need to have an unlimited checkbook. Sometimes just your loving thoughts will suffice.

The things that you create in the current lifetime are important to the development of the soul, but the spirit is veiled about the information that the soul contains. Why might this be you might be asking? The guides have explained that each experience can have a different twist and that your evolution depends on the ability of the soul to collect a variety of experiences. It is not the spirits job to analyze the experiences of the soul, so it becomes veiled.

In the afterlife, there will be better perception of important emotions such as compassion, love, and forgiveness. In the physical body, it is not so easy to feel these things because one is further from the soul. True compassion comes from deep within the spirit. True love comes from deep within the soul. True forgiveness comes from the infinite mind.

Chapter 4 – Your Spirit's Functions

The spirit has five main functions. Certainly, it has hundreds altogether, but these are the principal ways in which it functions. This chapter will also explain what to do when your spirit is not functioning well. Functions are the abilities the spirit uses to help you obtain your soul's purpose.

1. Desire
2. Thought
3. Comprehension
4. Reasoning
5. Self-Worth

Desire

Desire is the first function of the spirit. Desire, in this case, is defined specifically as your will to help people. It's not your basic desires like hunger and sex—your physical body drives those. In the spiritual sense, desire is the motor that propels our spirit.

The way a person chooses to assist others is a form of desire. For example, you may choose to have children, tell jokes, or be an astronaut. Not everything in life is as important or relevant to a spirit's form of desire. Career may be important, and marriage irrelevant, or vice-versa. Maybe neither career nor family matters, but just brightening the day of random others with goofy jokes. There is no telling how a spirit has chosen to manifest its desire to help others.

Sometimes the impact of your desires may be larger than you would think. For instance, the joy someone may experience while lovingly tending a garden moves into the human mass consciousness, influencing others to feel joy in general or an appreciation of plants as well. You may think your life may not amount to much because of how your culture defines success, but you may be a powerful influence through your lovingness.

The more you focus on your spirit's desires, the stronger your connection is to your spirit and the more successful your life will be. This is because the good deeds that you accomplish build wealth of spirit. This is a higher form of wealth than simply money. Wealth is richness in your life, whether it's friends, family, peace, mental & physical health, good times, etc. The manifestation of wealth becomes easier because of your stronger connection to your spirit.

Thought

Thought—as a function of the spirit—has nothing to do with memory, distorted societal beliefs, or mundane Earthly details. Rather, thought is dealing with your soul directives. Spiritual thought couldn't care less whether your clothes match or where you left your watch. Spiritual thought is the pathway to your soul's demands; it is the constant connection, keeping track of what you should be doing.

Interestingly, all thinking occurs outside of the physical body. It might be a hard concept to grasp for most people, but your body is a collection of cells that function as a unit to keep you alive. In actuality, your spirit connects electrically to the neural pathways in your brain, which triggers the perception of your spirit's thoughts in your brain. If you think about it that way, it's not so hard to understand that your body is not doing the thinking but is responding to the thought process from the spirit. No matter how injured the physical body becomes, the mind still has the ability to think, which is often described in near-death experiences. In the case of stroke victims, for example, their neural pathways have lost their electrical connection to the spirit. In fact, you can kill the body and the thinking process will continue. Your spirit continues to think on into the afterlife.

Comprehension

Comprehension is the ability to organize the things you perceive into a structure for learning. In other words, you make sense of what you see based upon what you know. For example, if you and a boat-maker both look at a boat, the boat-maker will have a much deeper comprehension of the boat. The boat maker will better be able to evaluate it identifying details of the boat's structure, age and integrity. You, on the other hand, will evaluate the boat from the more limited perspective of someone who has only seen and ridden in boats. This, basically, is comprehension. Your spirit provides this ability for you to understand the many facets in life: how things work, relationships, languages, compassion, and beyond.

Reasoning

Reasoning is the process of forming conclusions, judgments, and inferences from facts or premises. This is how one may decide what is right and wrong.

Like thinking, reasoning is not done in the brain; the brain can't function in that way. Reasoning is only done at the spiritual level. The brain is just the physical matter that moves our signals to our cells, like the hardware in a computer. Reasoning can be confused with consciousness or thinking. If a spirit has poor reasoning, then people make the comment that the person has no consciousness. This is a misnomer, because all spirit has consciousness and what people are really talking about is the lack of *reasoning* in the spirit. To be able to reason, there must first be a desire, then a thought, then comprehension of that thought.

Self-Worth

Self-worth as a function of the spirit is the result of the level of success achieved in the first four functions of the spirit. A spirit builds its self-worth by both positive and negative experiences. One would think that a person would only benefit from the positive experiences in life. However, the spirit makes no distinction between positive and negative experiences. This distinction is a forced cultural idea that does nothing to build self-worth.

Perhaps you've experienced hardships where later, you can see you've become stronger, matured because of having to work through those difficulties. In the middle of these hardships, it's difficult to see the value of your struggle. Your success from both negative and positive experiences builds self-worth. The spirit wants nothing more than to build self-worth. After the self-worth builds, the spirit will judge itself at the end of each incarnation. The spirit, not the soul, does the judging.

Nourishing Your Spirit, Finding Your Purpose

One might wonder whether spirits become weak. According to my spirit guides, a spirit's energy remains constant. For example, spirits, never feel hungry or tired. In fact, you they feel many of the human emotions. Although this might seem disturbing at first, consider this: most of our emotions come not from our spirits, but from our bodily needs. There is no reason for a spirit to experience fear since it cannot die or to feel sadness as it is so connected to your soul.

Although your spirit never goes 'hungry,' it is still important to nourish it. If you do not nourish your spirit, you are just existing and not adding much to your soul development. Most books on success and wealth completely disregard nourishment of the spirit. To nourish your spirit, you should do things that are in alignment with your soul's purpose. How do you know what your soul's purpose is? This is a common question I am asked when I am doing healings or readings. When you nourish your spirit, you will become closer to your spirit and your soul's mission will become more evident. The mission of your soul is not to accumulate wealth, as some people may think. It's not important to drive a Mercedes or look a certain way. Fundamentally, there are four ways you can nourish your spirit and find your purpose: you can **experience**, **love**, **create**, and **reproduce**.

So, what does this mean? First: **experience** the world and the people in it. Traveling the world can be great for the spirit. Anyone can be a tourist; what it really takes is talking to others, learning about other cultures, and seeing new ways to interact. Yet, you don't have to travel to experience. If you're involved in a community, with the people around you, you are experiencing. It may be through socializing that you will meet other people that may help you nourish your spirit. The spirit is also nourished through discovering and learning new things and giving yourself time for experiences pleasurable to your spirit.

It is important to **love** others. Love doesn't just mean affection; you have love when you are helping or appreciating others. Through love, there is much nourishing. People confuse sex with love; although sex can bring about bonding, it does not directly nourish the spirit.

What does it mean to **create**? In the context of spiritual nourishment, it's about improving the world around us. This is a form of love, indirectly. For example, when I was young, I started a business in manufacturing. This was creating by providing jobs for others. Doing things like this—creating for others—is a fundamental way to nourish your spirit. This can be accomplished in many ways, including teaching, building, cleaning, and volunteering. You might invent something, develop something that wasn't available before, or simply improve on what already exists. Being creative can just be the style you choose in interacting with others. If you're doing your part to help others, you're helping your spirit. Nothing kills your spirit more than a lack of creativity.

Reproduction may seem obvious; many of us have children, and it may not feel that special. However, reproduction spiritually does not simply refer to having your own children. Reproduction, in a spiritual sense, is about continuing our people and our Earth for future generations. To nourish your spirit, you may also plant trees or other greenery. For example, my grandfather felt nourished through his planting of evergreen trees. He felt that our home state of North Dakota needed more pines. However, pines take a long time to grow, so he knew that he would not live to see the trees fully grown. For him however, it wasn't about the final product. It was about reproducing, about paying forward to future generations who would benefit from the full-grown pines. His grandchildren continue to farm his land, and they can appreciate the trees.

There are members of society that ignore reproduction; for example, the slaughtering of rainforests has contributed to the demise of many species. It is upsetting the balance of nature. Other members are quite concerned about our environment and spend a lot of time in their lives with reproduction. I like the sustainable school of thought that espouses "Harvest a tree, plant a tree."

Fundamentally, all four ways to nourish one's spirit are about being creative. The reason for this is simple: the Universal Creator gave us the mission of being co-creators. When we co-create, we advance our species. It may feel daunting to learn this; you may likely feel like you don't even know what you're meant to create, much less that you might be a co-creator with the creator of the Universe. Just being alive, you add your unique perspective to the world; those around you would not be the same without you. You are free to add to the creation of life in any form you want.

The more someone focuses on nourishing the spirit, the more fulfilling their lives tend to be. In addition, the more fulfilling their lives are, the faster time seems to move. If you don't like what you're doing, days can seem to take forever. If it feels like a boring repetitive thing, if time seems like it's always moving slowly, you're not doing anything nourishing to your spirit.

The Malnourished Spirit

A malnourished spirit contributes to a malnourished soul. Your spirit will feel malnourished if you aren't living a life filled with at least one of the four nourishing avenues. A majority of problems in life stem from having a malnourished spirit. Sometimes people choose to bury themselves in bad habits, and this causes problems unto themselves. However, people may choose these habits in the first place to hide from their malnourished spirit. This can lead to the physical body becoming ill: depressed, overweight, physically malnourished, and lethargic. People may quit exercising, quit experiencing life, and seem to just waste away. It's important to consider that when you see negative traits in other people, it's not necessarily due entirely to laziness, bad genes, or bad luck. If you were to look deeper, you might see that they need spiritual nourishment. Often, nourishing the spirit helps address many of the obvious struggles people face.

Lacking love, due to holding grudges towards others, creates malnourishment in the spirit. Anger and hatred can also be hard on physical health. The spirit can see a much larger perspective, and it tries to convince the conscious mind to forgive.

Society has developed psychologists, life coaches, and other therapists who help you get to the core of your problems. At the core, you will find your spirit. You must identify the problem, in order to find what your spirit has been prodding us to do.

The best way to help someone is to discover what he or she came here to do. What is their mission? Some people claim that they have no clue what their mission is. These people need the most help. Finding your mission doesn't mean you have to give up your family or your high-paying job. It means you need to find a balance in your life, to enjoy doing things that fulfill your spirit. The more you pay attention to what fulfills your spirit, the closer you will sense what your soul's mission or purpose is.

Fear and doubt are two of the biggest hindrances to finding one's mission. When the physical body becomes fearful, it weakens the connection to the spirit. Fear is a big barrier to spiritual development. For example, I've lost so many friends in my lifetime that I have a natural fear of losing a friendship. Anyone who has gone through a divorce can probably relate to this fear. Divorce is painful, like losing a friend in death, and they both are quite damaging to the personality. If the fear comes too close to the surface, you will push away friends because you automatically attract more of what is coming to mind. It does not matter to the spirit if you are thinking about something negative or positive. It will be damaging to you if you project any fear into the Universe. You do not mean to bring fear to the forefront, but unless you learn to cope with the traumas in your life, you will attract experiences you may not want. Fear keeps you further from your spirit by limiting your options to grow.

The spirit has no doubt, but the personality does. We doubt the things we read. We doubt what people say. We doubt ourselves, and doubt gets in the way if we are trying to learn something new. Doubt is like brick, and the wall that doubt creates can become a roadblock to life. I think about the things that I doubt every day, and I am quite aware that I should not do this. Almost everyone I meet is a 'doubting Thomas' in some way. If we are following our spirit, we will not experience doubt. The spirit world suggests that we should address our sources of doubt to alleviate them.

Self-doubt is the most common type of doubt. Another is not being able to trust other people. The last—and most difficult to overcome—is not being able to trust the Universe; that is, not having faith that the Universe wants to help you and that you can receive help from the Universe if you ask. I asked the spirit world, other than the hindrances due to fear and doubt, why are people so unhappy in the world? Their answer was that people aren't doing anything to nourish the spirit. In order for life to be exciting, there needs to be balance between mundane survival and activities that nurture the spirit. If you do the same thing repeatedly, and don't care for your job or your activities, the spirit can get restless. The main reason that I found for people not doing any exciting things in their lives is that they believe they can afford neither the money nor the time. Tell the Universe what you want and watch the ways in which it manifests. It may also help by doing your part by seeing where you waste your money or energy. Many have been convinced by mass advertising to purchase things that they do not need. These things complicate living conditions and just add to the confusion of life. I know I am guilty of this. My vinyl record collection has grown to such a size that I couldn't possibly listen to it all.

The easiest way to align yourself with spirit is to engage in activities that inspire you. Many of you have jobs that you may not find inspirational but are effective in paying the bills. You cannot expect to make a clear connection to your spirit guides if you are not participating in inspiring activities. Through my years of providing healing work, I have found people who have not discovered much that is inspiring to them, yet they yearn for inspiration. Inspiration does not land in your lap; you have to cultivate areas of interest and do your share of research. I have been surprised at some of the things that I have found to be inspiring. For example, as a young boy growing up, I had no idea I would enjoy archaeological information. Now I find archaeology a fascinating subject. We all have the need to explore different topics. Some topics may light fires under us and others will not.

When you take a job solely for the money, it may work for a while, but eventually, events will occur that seem to push you away from that job. Perhaps the fear of poverty has kept you stuck in a dead-end job. I once saw an interview of a man who had just recently won the lottery. When asked what he was going to do with the money, he said he didn't know, but he had already decided that he was going to quit his job. You can ask yourself this same question: if I won the lottery, would I keep my job? If the answer is no—and in most cases, it is—then I would venture a guess that your spirit isn't in alignment with that job. I'm not suggesting that people quit their jobs simply because they don't like them. What I am suggesting is that you find some things to do that are inspiring. Perhaps the job is just a temporary stepping-stone. While you're looking for another avenue to make a living that brings you closer to your spirit, make time somewhere in your week to do inspiring activities to nurture your spirit. Maybe it is reading a book, bike-riding, or visiting friends. Anything that inspires you will help bring you closer to your spirit and energize your life for new doors to open.

People who do not feel inspired in their lives often turn to addictions to cover up their pain. This is even less inspiring for the spirit as the spirit knows that addictions do not provide real happiness. However, the personality does not understand that addictions distance you from your spirit. You are still connected to the spirit but are not getting anything out of your life. Your agreement to incarnate was a contract that I refer to as a 'soul contract'. One might ask how can one remember our soul contract if it is masked by addictions? The answer is that you don't. Note: temporary addictions can be useful, if they give you first-hand knowledge about some of the hardships of the human condition.

Your spirit understands much more than your personality does. However, this does not mean that your personality is a lower self or is less important than our spirit. Your personality is something that develops, grows, and the older we get, the more apparent our likes and dislikes become. Your personality never stops developing, and your interests continuously change.

The Malnourished Spirit in Practice

People often feel as though there just isn't enough time in the day but when I ask people to walk through their day, I'm surprised to find how many have free hours devoted to 'rest.' That is, anything that isn't directly related to work or family. This rest time includes a variety of things such as watching television, drinking, smoking, or simply sitting around. It is in these times that people could find spirit-nourishing activities instead. After all, you already commit time to your work and family; shouldn't you commit time to your spirit as well? When it is nourishing to your spirit, it will feel more like rest than work.

If you want to transition to a new career, you can do it in small steps. You need to first know what you want and then plan how you can successfully transition to the new job or career. Let's say that you are employed at a great law firm, and you really wanted to be a dancer. You aren't sure what kind of living a dancer could make, so you first investigate the options. Possibly, you could join a recreational dance troupe and have some fun. The way you earn a living doesn't always have to be your first love. It is also important to realize that just because you enjoy a hobby doesn't mean that you would enjoy doing it full-time.

If you're looking for a spirit-nourishing hobby or career, know that you're not alone. If you have forgotten what your spirit likes, look back to interests you had as a child when you were more aligned with your spirit. You shouldn't necessarily hang out in a sandbox but think hard about your past interests. These interests are often more descriptive of your core passions. You can also ask your heart in a sense, what types of things would you be involved in if there were no hindrances. Just play with the ideas for a while.

Sometimes we are concerned how we will appear to others and are afraid to be our true selves. I was afraid for many years even to write this book. I was afraid that someone would judge me or not understand who I am. Who is this guy, who thinks he can talk to spirit guides? He should be put into a strait jacket. Nevertheless, by not writing the book and not following my spirit, I was putting myself into my own strait jacket. I knew that the only opinion that matters is my own, but I went around worrying about what others thought of me. That is an insecure trait and I'm glad I'm not my old self. My new self is looking forward to each new day. I certainly have tough days just like anyone else, but I can see the light at the end of the tunnel. It is a huge tunnel just filled with light.

All experiences are gifts to the spirit. Your personality gets bored with the same old thing. Many people change careers not because the personality wants to, but because the spirit is getting nothing from it. The way to have a happy life is to give the spirit something to chew on. It needs nourishment and it needs stimulating experiences.

A Liberated Spirit

Therefore, what is the upshot of all this? The spirit's final goal—its most fundamental—is to help the spirit become liberated. To liberate the spirit the spirit must first master desire, then thought, then comprehension, then reasoning. Lastly, they must build their self-worth to a point that they have completed the self-actualization process. It is a process because it can take many lifetimes to achieve. A self-actualized spirit has developed a full, clear connection to its soul. Once the soul has achieved a self-actualized spirit, it is then, liberated in that dimension. The soul then sends a spirit to the next dimension. It will usually choose a higher dimension and not the other way around.

Once a spirit is liberated from all twelve dimensions, it can unite with the Master Creator. It can stay in the Macroscopic Realm, or it can decide to reenter one of the other dimensions of the twelve-dimensional cycle again. A liberated spirit has been through the struggles of incarnations and has had so many vital experiences, so it would mainly back to return to assist others. It may want to experience life on the same planet that it has already mastered but would like to experience the new technologies since its last incarnation or help with the creative process.

Many advanced spirits have been around the circle of life (the twelve dimensions) numerous times. Because the dimensions are connected in a circular fashion, the soul can send a spirit to enter a dimension anywhere on the circle once it has achieved liberation. A new spirit will normally begin its journey through the circle of life in the 1st of the twelve dimension, whereas a liberated soul can send a spirit down into any of the dimensions. At this point, the spirit may choose a role in the dimension that it believes needs assistance. It may come down to help a soul family advance or help its soul group or others in general.

A liberated spirit takes on a role like that of an angel; in each case, liberated spirits and angels are both helping others evolve spiritually. The major difference: a liberated spirit takes on a body. Have you met anyone who seems to be like an angel, but is as physical as can be? If you have, chances are this is a liberated spirit. Someone may refer to a person as having a liberated spirit. The term *liberated spirit* usually refers to a person who appears to be happy, fully accepting themselves and freely being their true spirit.

A person with a liberated spirit may not even be consciously aware that that they have been liberated. The best way to find out whether your spirit is liberated is to connect with your guides or angels and ask them. This is not some great secret. If you have a sincere desire to help humanity in some way, then chances are you are one of those people.

You may wonder: why would a spirit want to leave the Master Creator? Certainly, they want to help others; but sometimes the soul wants further incarnations so it can still enjoy new experiences. Just because a spirit has been liberated does not mean it has experienced everything. With each incarnation, it sees new societies. Some spirits want to relearn because new technologies are providing experiences that the soul wishes to have. Remember, life does not just occur on Earth, it occurs on many planets across all Universes. A liberated spirit may not have chosen a mission to evolve by itself, but specifically to evolve with others. A liberated spirit helps others become liberated.

Chapter 5 – The Celestial Realm

While doing healings across the United States, I've found that people have many different beliefs about where we go after we die. Some call it Heaven, while others call it the afterlife. To the spirit world, it is known as the Celestial Realm. Plato originally used the term "celestial," and he used the term the way the spirit world is teaching us.

So just what is the Celestial Realm? The Celestial Realm contains the 4th, 5th and 6th dimensions. In this book, it isn't relevant to learn in-depth information about the 4th and 5th dimensions; our souls tend only to reside in the 6th dimension. We'll cover just a brief description of the 4th and 5th dimensions.

The 4th dimension is often referred to as the 'astral plane.' When the spirit leaves the body during astral travel, it can view the 4th dimension. The 4th dimension is abundant with life forms known as celestial beings. These celestial beings include such things as nature spirits, fairies, leprechauns, and similar beings that some consider mythological. Yet you may know people who believe they see these beings. They may not be bluffing; rarely, people can peer into the 4th dimension.

Other 4th dimensional life forms are so different from humans; they may seem scary or overwhelming. Some examples are ghouls, goblins and beings that do not have actual physical bodies as we do. However, there is no need to worry about 4th dimensional danger, the separation of the realms makes it difficult for them to impact us. Ghost are spirits that have separated from their physical body but for various reasons are stuck in between the 3rd and 4th dimensions.

If the spirit chooses to go deeper into the Celestial Realm, it will head to a tunnel. This tunnel starts in the 4th dimension, and is a shortcut to the 6th dimension, where our souls reside. Going through this tunnel is a wild ride that will feel familiar to everyone. It feels like you are being bathed in white energy while traveling at enormous speeds. It is far beyond the speed of light. Once entering the tunnel, the spirit is not able to turn back in midstream, as the force is too strong. However, in the case of near-death experiencers, they are allowed by a divine design to turn back.

It can return through the tunnel only after reaching the end, as I did when I re-entered my body from my afterlife experience.

The 5th dimension is where entities of a higher level of consciousness reside. Here, 5th dimensional beings have their own planetary systems. Incarnates in the 5th dimension have a light-body form and have the ability to astral project at will and travel through the cosmos. They appear solid-like to each other. We cannot travel to the 5th dimension with a spacecraft, but our spirits can go there.

For those of you that have been told that Earth is moving into the 5th dimension, I am sorry to inform you that it is quite unlikely. Quantum researchers have hypothesized that an act like that would likely destroy the entire Universe. Although the Master Creator is capable of moving Earth to another dimension it has never happened before. Rather, the *awareness* of the people is shifting to a higher level.

I once had a brief encounter in the 5th dimension. It differed from the physical realm experience in multiple ways, but the primary way was that time and space were not constant. For instance, when traveling fifty miles an hour on Earth, it feels like a specific speed. Whereas in the 5th dimension, fifty miles an hour could feel like moving at varying speeds. Another example is that someone can be half a mile away, but sound up close when talking. Also in the 5th dimension, a lot of communicating is done telepathically through a part of our mind called a *perometer*. This can be opened to let us hear telepathically, but my guides have not informed me how to do this yet. It is not that it would be a physical strain on my body, but perhaps it has more to do with being an invasion of people's private thoughts.

In the 3rd dimensional experience, your astral body can leave, and you may experience an altered state of consciousness. By this, I mean your conscious mind may not remember anything, but it may have recorded the experience. It might be recalled through hypnosis. The astral body cannot be destroyed, so there's little risk of making mistakes that could lead to a death or injury.

The 6th dimension is where your spirits spend most of its time when you're not incarnated. It is not necessary to stop at the 5th dimension in order to get to the 6th dimension, the spirit would use the tunnel of light from the 4th dimension to the sixth. This white-light tunnel transports our spirits beyond the speed of light, to a place that is billions of light-years away. The 4th and 5th dimensions are closer to the Earth, but you cannot perceive their frequencies.

The 6th dimension is made up of seven levels. All dimensions include multiple levels, but you will be primarily focus on those within the 6th dimension. I was able to see most of these levels during my afterlife experience. When you are looking at the stars in the sky, you are really seeing the 3rd dimensional aspect of the 6th dimension. It is almost impossible for you to understand just how vast the 6th dimension is. The entire Universe is just a speck in comparison to the celestial realm.

My Brush with the Afterlife

As I mentioned, in my youth I had a afterlife experience. One night in college, I drank heavily with a friend and passed out. The next morning, my friend tried to wake me up for class. He noticed I had gone cold. He was still drunk and was worried that he would be charged with contributory negligence; so he left me be. As it turned out, I had died. He was gone for the day with classes, and when he returned that night, he found me still cold. He was sure I was dead.

When I came to, I found him with his head in his hands, worried about the situation. He was shocked to see me come walking out. He told me I had been cold for more than twelve hours. I didn't tell him, but from my perspective, I'd been gone for days. Time is irrelevant in the celestial realm. From this, I have retained a first-hand understanding of what the celestial realm truly is. Let me lay to rest any misunderstandings about the 6th dimension you've possibly heard. People refer to the 6th dimension as Heaven, but Heaven is more like an introduction to the 6th dimension. There *is* a Heaven, but it's only the waiting room before you enter the 6th dimension.

The spirit guides have described the 6th dimension as being divided into seven fundamental levels to facilitate our understanding. They all flow smoothly together, making it hard to say where exactly one ends, and another begins.

Sixth Dimension I - Principium

The first level, principium is my favorite, because it's the part of the 6th dimension that can be seen from Earth at night. You are just getting a glimpse of the outer crust of Principium when you stare into the sky. If you gaze at the stars, you may get the strong notion, there is something greater out there. Some of the lights you see are just reflections of the outer shell of Principium. Principium is also one entrance to the tunnel of light that connects the 4th and 6th dimensions. If you think this sounds Latin, you are right, because the word translated means "basic principle," which is an appropriate term for the outermost level of the 6th dimension. I don't think a google search will come up with terms that my guides use for these levels, but they are useful to help explain the model.

Sixth Dimension II - Proximus

Proximus is the second level of the 6th dimension and as you might have guessed, it is a Latin term for the next level. It can be translated as, "nearest." This is perceived as a white light, for people who remember their near-death experience. I call this tunnel the shortcut from the 4th to the 6th dimension. When I experienced Proximus, I thought perhaps people who use the word ascension might really be referring to this process. There is such a strong feeling that your spirit is ascending somewhere but at the time, you don't really comprehend where you are heading to, and it would appear there is no turning back.

Proximus is a bright, spiritually uplifting place. Here, spirits float through energy, surrounded by light. The light refracts into brilliant hues, and there is a sensation of traveling at very high speed. Yet the speed isn't scary because the realm is so comforting, so uplifting. Warm, welcoming energy surrounds spirits here, drawing them toward the light through a tunnel.

In my near-death experience, the level of Proximus felt real. In Proximus, one may feel even more real than when in the physical realm. There is also a familiarity to this place, which only makes sense; your spirits have visited this place many times before, after your bodies died in previous lifetimes. There is also a comforting sense of certainty; in Proximus, you know you belong there. All the fears and doubts, the two things that hinder you the most, are gone. Proximus is a comfortable place where spirits go during a near-death experience.

During my time in Proximus, my mind was whirling in wonder and awe. I found that space is not a void but is instead comprised of vast dimensions that you don't access while you are alive.

Sixth Dimension III - Medius

The next level is called *Medius*. It come from the Latin word meaning middle. I like to think of this as the resting place of the soul, what many religions refer to as Heaven. The Bible calls Heaven the "New Jerusalem." Of course, it also states that only God's chosen people get to go there and that everyone else goes to hell. However, the fact of the matter is this: we all go to Medius when we die.

It may be surprising, but I never found hell at any level. It may be surprising to hear this, and perhaps a little concerning. If we all go to Medius, what stops us from doing terrible things on Earth? It is simply this:

each of us can create Hell wherever we live, and many people do. Hell doesn't exist; it's about a person's perception of an experience.

Could this information cause people to go out and murder one another? Religions thought this was the case, therefore the model of Heaven and Hell became quite popular as a control mechanism for years. Religious leaders thought it was for the peoples own good. Perhaps times were different in the past, but from what I see in the news, the murdering has not stopped on the account of a false religious belief. So what good is a false religious belief if it only keeps you further from the truth?

I would argue that if everyone learned that we all go to Medius, only then would we all recognize that we are eternal beings and live our lives peacefully. Only then would violence become unnecessary. On many advanced civilizations on other planets, crime is nearly unheard of. That is because these civilizations understand the spiritual implications of life better than we do.

When I first arrived in Medius, it felt like the traditional description of Heaven. That is, there are 'many rooms,' as Jesus said. There are multitudes of places in Medius, each with a specific peaceful scene. I went from place to place in Medius, and in each place, I experienced whatever peaceful thing that came to my mind. For instance, when I thought about Jesus, then an entity came forward that I recognized instantly as him. When I asked him questions, I got instant answers without even having any verbal communication.

I loved it in Medius. I didn't have any desire to go back to my body, but I was told by my spirit guides and Jesus, that I had much work yet to do. Does it surprise you that Jesus was there? It should not, because Jesus is a master teacher and master guide, and resides in even higher levels in the Celestial Realm. I was surprised when Jesus waved his hand over me, and my questions were answered instantly. I knew that I had to go back and do the things I had agreed to do. Since I was young when I had my near-death experience, I had accomplished little at that point.

Jesus told me that we are representative of the Master Creator. We are cut from the same cloth, because the Master Creator made the Universal creator, who in turn made us. I asked whether it was acceptable to worship the Master Creator. Jesus said that we could be *reverent* to deities, but that we should not *worship* deities. Furthermore, he said that it is not right to worship Jesus himself. Jesus did not incarnate so that we may worship him. It is true that we will not get to God except through Jesus, but that is because God is at a higher level than where Jesus resides. Jesus is one of the few that can access all thirteen dimensions at will. I asked Jesus, "When I return to Earth, what church do I join?" He said, "None of them." Churches are organized as businesses, and to speak to God we simply communicate with the superconscious mind. The superconscious mind connects directly to the soul, and the soul transmits information on to the Universal Creator. Therefore, it is through us that we can talk to God—that is, our Universal Creator. For all practical purposes, our Universal Creator is as high up the chain of command as our communication could go. Only the Universal Creator communicates with the Master Creator.

When we pray to God, our prayers are answered by two routes. In some instances, the universal laws of thought come into play attracting and creating the reality that is representative of the thoughts that we have. This is discussed in more detail in part II of the book. In other cases, the message is sent out to the Universe and is dealt with by a chain of command. Our spirit guides, guardian angel, and others in the angelic realm who have the relevant abilities will be called on to assist. It is fine to pray to God, but know it is not God directly who will be assisting.

Sixth Dimension IV - Quartus

The next level of the celestial realm is called Quartus. As soon as I reached Quartus, it felt familiar. I thought to myself, *I know this place*. At first, I was amazed at the colors and the wonderful meadow I was standing in. There was no temperature, and no sensations like on Earth, but somehow it felt warm and soft. Every flower and blade of grass seemed perfect. Everything in this realm appeared untainted. I no longer felt negative emotions.

I wondered what spirits did here, because it was so beyond comprehension of the physical plane. I met with my father guide at that moment. This is the guide who stays with you throughout your lifetime so is referred to as the father guide since this spirit stays with you your entire lifetime, so this spirit is much like a father in that sense. My father guide explained to me that in Quartus, I would be able to remember my physical life, and be able to recognize the spirits of others. The purpose of Quartus is to give us the space to review our lives. As I mentioned previously, we are the judges of our own lives. It is also, where the spirit is re-energized after having an exhausting, earthly body.

Though the purpose of Quartus might imply that it would be foreboding, due to the judgment of one's life, this couldn't be farther from the truth. Quartus is a place of communion and of great joy. As the physical plane is a place to develop the individual spirit, this is a place to strengthen and develop the soul. It is also a preparatory stage where the soul can develop what it wants the spirit to be in the next life. Here you work with your spirit guides to choose a personality for your next incarnation.

The key to spiritual progress is to follow the path that you outlined for yourself. My guide asked if I wanted to see my path, and of course, I said yes. I saw visions of what I could be doing in the future. I saw myself with children, even though I wasn't married at the time. I saw myself working in a building with my family—but not on the farm. At that stage in my life, I had figured that I would first finish college and return to farming with my father and brother. I could see that I would be working with people in their healing, and later, as a teacher giving workshops about the spiritual world. It was amazing, to see what I was going to be doing in my life and I then realized that my life had hardly even begun.

At the time, I was a musician in a band so I thought I could do one of two things. I could focus on the music career or go into the field of agriculture. In my afterlife experience, I didn't know for sure what I would choose but it seemed logical to choose music as a hobby. Looking back on it now, I realized that I needed to get away from my comfortable life choice. Therefore, I took a leap of faith and choose a third option that I had not anticipated. I went into business as a manufacturer and I made money doing it, but the act was for me, hollow. I knew I wasn't on Earth for that purpose either.

While I was in Quartus, my father guide was at my side. I couldn't see him directly—but I could feel his presence. During my time there, it seemed like he was there to answer my every question. I asked my guide if he was my only guide.

"Well, no," he answered. He explained to me that we all have more than one guide. He elaborated that some guides come to us only in specific situations or for certain reasons. Many guides would love to assist us in any way they can, but the father guide must first clear them. "I will be your guide throughout your life," this spirit explained.

Then, my father guide led me to a place where I could do a soul-life review. I was able to see some of my past lives and I was surprised how long I had been around. What shocked me the most was that we have lived in all dimensions and have lived countless lives?

I was excited to have such clarity about myself, so I asked about previous lives. I saw so many lives flashing before me. I had lived in difficult times, during important times in history; I lived on other planets, and in other Universes. In one life, I was a teacher. In another, I was a medical doctor. I was a concubine once and a great leader in another time. I realized that we all live a huge variety of lives, ranging from great leaders to simple folk. Our souls all get a wide range of experiences during our lifetimes.

I was somewhat more influential in some of the previous lives, and I wondered why? Am I regressing in my importance? Each of our lives determines its place in the hierarchy, so it's not as if one always gets more advanced in each lifetime. Each life is entirely independent of the others, and they occur in a period for which we have no concept.

As I watched scenes from past lives, I understood why I was attracted to some things and desired to avoid others. For instance, I've always had a terrible fear of falling to my death. In my soul-life review, I learned that I had died previously from falling. I am also afraid of snakes; sure enough, I'd been killed by a poisonous snake. I've always been attracted to fishing, particularly in the Mediterranean. Fishing has always seemed so 'sensible' to me. Turns out, I was once a Mediterranean angler.

I get asked a lot when I am doing readings on people if a previous life can affect the current one. Since they are independent of one another, and you remember so little about your past lives. I would think the answer would be no but, there are those who can remember small details and it might cause a certain phobia. I have run into cases where people that may have a fear of water may have drowned in a previous life but of course, they would have to remember this in one of the three minds for it to affect the current life.

I asked my spirit guide whether I would be able to remember my past lives more clearly now if I decided to go back to the physical realm. I knew that I had not been completed my mission. He said that I would remember a few things but not all the details. He said that those lives were no longer important, and what was important was what I would do with the life I was now living.

I did agree that in my current life I was feeling unfulfilled, and I seemed to be on a dead-end road. My guide explained that in time I would do more with my healing gift and would be channeling messages for people from the spirit world.

At first, I thought he meant words from the deceased, but he explained that it was messages for humanity, and that I had agreed to be a liaison between the spirit world and the physical realm. At that time, I was anxious to begin. He told me that there was no hurry to become those things. I had to first receive a traditional education and spend some time with my family.

I asked when I would become a healer. He told me that I could do it at any time, but that it would not be my livelihood. He told me that, first, I had to meet my soul group.

I was excited about meeting my soul group. It was eighteen years before my daughter would be born and I remember that moment as if it just happened a few years ago. There was a spark of recognition that moment I saw her. I knew I had just met someone from my soul group. It was such a happy feeling, and I realized then that my life was getting purpose. It was a sign that I was on the right path. About two years later, my son was born, and I knew my family was complete. That had been the most satisfying time of my life up to that point, but I knew that there would be more to come. I just didn't know when.

I didn't become a professional healer for several years, after the time when my two children were young. I focused on my children but was also concerned about the possibility of using my healing as a career. I thought that, surely, healing wouldn't be able to support a family. It wasn't until much later—and perhaps for the best—that I returned to working more deeply with my guides and healing.

Sixth Dimension V - Eduction

I told my Father spirit guide I wanted to see the next level. He took me to a place that my spirit guides called Eduction. He explained this was the place of the enlightened ones. He explained the enlightened ones, are a council of spirits that review lives. They don't judge us, but they do help you choose your pathway. Here, you learn more about your personal weaknesses and your successes.

In Eduction, you receive an education about not only your own experiences, but also how your experiences fit in with others'. You see how your experiences compare to others so that you may know how you relate to the universal scheme of things. It was obvious, for example, how the planets affect each other. At the time, it all seemed to make perfect sense. Unfortunately, when I returned to my physical body, I couldn't remember the relationships. This is an example of 'soul memory'—the soul retains a memory, but the conscious mind can't hold on to it.

Of course, I wanted to see the enlightened ones, and in a flash, I was there. Yet it wasn't a room, because there were no floors or walls. Before me were seated large beings on huge chairs. I was seeing them through with my spirit vision. They appeared regal and human, but so magnificent that I could not speak. They communicated with me telepathically and I seemed to respond telepathically. They seemed to want to know why I was there in Eduction; they thought I had a life to continue. It seemed that I was trying to argue my way in, that I didn't want to return to my body.

Although I disagreed, I did not feel afraid, as there were no emotions in Eduction. I sensed that there was something bigger going on, and I realized that I'd been here before, asking to be incarnated again.

I was judging myself! It was another *'Aha'* moment for me, because I realized then that no one judges us. We judge ourselves. However, that shattered my perception because I thought the Bible was at least right that God judges us. I know now that we judge ourselves much more harshly than God ever would. The things that they had me envision were too complex to put into words. I had no business going to the next two levels. I knew then that I needed to return to my physical body.

At this point, I chose to go back to my body. I thought there would be a process, steps I had to take to get back. However, shockingly, I was thrown back into the physical realm instantly. I awoke from my drunken coma, without a hangover. I felt better than I had in years, as the first five levels of the celestial realm had been a great spiritual cleansing.

Sixth Dimension VI - Provectus

The enlightened beings from Eduction had told me there were two more levels of the 6th dimension, but it wasn't until later that my spirit guides finally educated me about them. The sixth level of the 6th dimension is called *Provectus* which is a Latin word for advanced. It is a level where our universal awareness is transformed. We become keenly aware of what the Universe is. Here, at Provectus, enlightened beings such as liberated souls can become spirit guides. Spirit guides primarily reside in Provectus; unliberated spirits do come and go but tend to prefer Medius.

When we hear people talking about 'ascension,' their spirits are just longing to reach Provectus. Provectus is where more enlightened spirits connect to their spiritual lineages—that is the other spirits in their soul groups. Here, spirits can see their soul's history. Provectus is the point at which all understandings start to mature, because it is here that we truly get a larger view of existence. As such, this is the level where self-actualization truly expands. An older soul may decide with its guides to go to the 10th dimension for further study in choosing the next incarnation.

Sixth Dimension VII - Absolutus

The last level in the celestial realm is Absolutus. This is where spirits learn directly about creator beings in the 11th & 12th dimensions and reach an awareness of all knowledge and all truth. This is a Latin word that means final. They are not with the creator beings but can understand them. This level is a training ground to prepare spirits to become creators themselves. Spirits may also choose not to enter Absolutus, but rather continue to be spirit guides in the 6th dimension. They may also move on to the Angelic Realm.

The difference between Provectus and Absolutus is therefore enormous. Provectus is about the self, and Absolutus is about all that exists. Some people say that this is where you will find Jesus, or the Christ consciousness. I saw him in Medius, but the guides' said Jesus is at all levels simultaneously. If you achieve Absolutus, you too can be in all the levels of the celestial realm at the same time.

Absolutus is so huge, so beyond our comprehension, that there aren't words to describe it. It's worth only mentioning, so that you know that—in time—you too may achieve Absolutus.

The Seven Levels in Review

There are seven different levels of the 6th dimension. Though the guides said that each could be further subdivided for this teaching, these seven levels are sufficient. The guides said that when people hear about the seven levels of the 6th dimension, their lives change because the knowledge will be more patterned, organized and simplified.

Knowing about the seven levels of the 6th dimension isn't just about finding comfort on Earth. Let this knowledge remind us that we are part of something much bigger than ourselves. We each have an important role to play. Keep these levels—and their sheer scale—in mind when we feel overwhelmed by life. Although it is easy to feel like our tiny problems are huge, they will seem like nothing when we return even to the lowest levels of the Celestial Realm.

In time, the importance of this fundamental information will begin permeating into and expanding your philosophy on life. The first five chapters were a warm-up. I am preparing you for some exciting information, but I understand if you need to take a break. Putting the book down temporarily is not going to hurt my feelings, but don't forget where you put it because it is just getting to get interesting.

Messages from the Spirit World

Chapter 6 - The Angelic Realm

I have always believed that angels are some of the most important beings in the Universe. As a child, I was taught about angels in the bible and most religions accept them but only a few people have claimed that they see angels. So where are all the angels? Did we lose the ability to communicate with them over time or did they just leave and go someplace else? Others may wonder, *are angels are really the product of an over-active imagination or did humankind just make them up*?

According to my spirit guides angels are beings of light that come from the angelic realm. When people make claims that angels are just messengers of God, and they serve no other purpose my guides are amused. They are even more amused when they hear people declare that angels have never lived as other beings. According to my spirit guides, nothing can be further from the truth. Angels can select to live in other dimensions, and they have souls just like beings in other dimensions.

The thing that I find the most fascinating about angels is that they are never at war with one another. He doesn't pick a fight with one another like we do on Earth. They have no judgment, no fear and none of the limiting negative emotions that humankind has. Angels have no need for adornment and when you pass out of your physical body, they are always there to greet you. They are perceived and not seen as we do with our physical eyes. Angels do not interfere with our daily lives and force us to do their bidding. They can be quite protective and help us stay on our life path but in no way do they have an agenda for us to follow. In this part, I will explain the function of the angels and from where they came.

The angelic realm is comprised of the 7th, 8th, and 9th dimensions. The angelic realm contains many highly evolved, loving beings other than angels. In the 7th dimension, the grouping of angels is referred to as "resident angels." These are the angels we see most often interacting in the lower dimensions. The 8th dimension contains the "guardian angels" and the 9th dimension is where the "archangels" reside.

The history books are full of references to angels. When you look at the angelic realm on the circle of life, can you not see that the Celestial Realm separates it? It is far removed from the Physical Realm. It is easy to see why there so few angel sightings are reported. We hear of people who claim they have seen ghosts, goblins, fairies, elves and extraterrestrial beings but these beings are much closer to the Physical Realm than angels are.

Few people actually talk about angels, and I was surprised about this fact. Although in my near-death experience I did not spend a great deal of time in the Angelic Realm, I witnessed it for a brief time. I was told that angels divinely intervene with the people of Earth, but they do not make themselves visible.

There have been numerous people who claim they feel the presence of angels but of course they will admit that they don't see them.

Angels can be our protectors and the moment that we call on them they respond if what we are asking them to do does not interfere negatively with our free will.

Those people who use black magic to influence others can call on angles but if their prayers have ill intent, the angels will ignore the prayers.

Resident Angels

This is the largest group of angels. These angels reside in the 7th dimension. In this book I will not go deeply into the angels because I helped co-author a book with Lisa Ulshafer that is titled, "Journey of an angel." Here I will make brief mention of the angels.

Some of the greatest prophets of all time have spoken about their understandings of resident angels. Numerous artists have painted, sculpted and dreamed of this group of angels. Have you ever noticed that most angels when painted by artists have wings? These are not resident angels according to my guides. When I had my afterlife experience, I saw plenty of angels, but I did not see any with wings. I wondered about that because in the Christian religion angels have wings. Most of my brief experience was in the 7th dimension and those angels did not have wings but my guides informed me that to earn your wings you would have to be of the highest order.

Occasionally angels decide to incarnate on Earth to assist humanity more directly. Incarnated angels directly enter physical form as a baby instead of going back to the 6th dimension and sending a spirit spark out to Earth. They often become musicians, writers, teachers and philanthropists of all sorts. They are usually noticed the most as famous musicians because angels are attracted to music and understand the profound impact it has on the spirit. In the book "Journey of an Angel," there is a chapter about famous incarnated angels.

Chapter 6 - The Angelic Realm

Guardian Angels

The 8th dimension is the home of the guardian angels, the second largest category of angels. Guardian angels work with people on a more individual basis than the resident angels. These angels have multiple assignments. They can be more interactive in the Physical Realm than a resident angel. There have been instances where a guardian angel has come to the aid of an individual who is facing certain death. The primary role of the guardian angel is to assist those resident angels in their missions.

In the 8th dimension, like the 5th dimension vibration is not a constant. You hear most sounds at approximately the same intensity. In the 8th dimension, the intensity can vary from one minute to the next. The distance that you are from the sound makes no difference in the intensity. Something that is a mile away can be just as obvious as something that is a few inches from our ear.

Angels from the 8th dimension see us in the 3rd dimension, but you are rarely able to see them. Lower vibrational forces rarely see higher vibrational forces. All beings in the Angelic Realm have only an energy body and lack a physical body. However, in their dimension, angels see each other and communicate much the same as we do in the Physical Realm.

The guardian angels receive data and information from the resident angels, and they receive their directives from a higher order that we call the *archangels*. The guardian angels do not interact with us as frequently as the resident angels do. Once a spirit becomes a guardian angel, they usually choose to move to a higher dimension rather than to incarnate to a lower dimensional frequency.

Guardian angels are often doing energy work all over the Universe. Since we are unable to see the guardian angels, it is hard to imagine the complexity of their role. The more guardian angels assigned to a particular planet, the more stable that planet will become.

Archangels

This is the highest and smallest group of angels, and they reside in the 9th dimension. They are the leaders or the masters of the angels. Not many come back to incarnate on the physical realm although it has happened on occasion. They generally are content to stay as leaders in the angelic realm to assist the other angels in their work. Archangels work with guardians and residents. They assign each resident to work with a guardian angel within this structured hierarchal system.

Archangels are the architects of the Angelic Realm. They are not the architects of the Universe, but they are the masters that control and shape the activities of the angelic realm. Rarely do these angels work with humans on a one-on-one basis due to the vastness of their responsibilities. The guardian and resident angels carry out those responsibilities. Frequently we will call on archangels for assistance, and these messages go directly to the resident angels and not to the archangels. It is possible for a message from a human to reach an archangel, but this rarely occurs.

Many people have claimed to be talking directly to archangels, if this was so, there would literally have to be billions of archangels. We know that there are not billions of archangels, as this is the smallest group in the angelic realm. There is no way for one archangel to answer billions of prayers simultaneously. This is why we have so many resident and guardian angels.

Other Angelics

These dimensions contain beings other than angels. Some of these beings may be confused with angels, but they are all high divine order. Some beings in the 7th dimension are master healers, and they come to us as apparitions occasionally. They are completely different from what you think of as ghosts. They are similar in vibration to extra-terrestrials in the 5th dimension but have a much different purpose for humanity. They might come to heal a person but are not involved in abductions.

Not all angels appear to be winged. Some appear like giant insects. These insectoid creatures belong to the Angelic Realm and are really "Mantis," as they look vaguely like human-sized praying mantis. Although their appearance may be foreboding, they are anything but dangerous. Just like angels, Mantis is likely some of the most helpful beings in the 7th dimension. The thing that is interesting about the 7th dimension is that the beings that reside there most often work in healing beings from all dimensions. They are often responsible for many healings that you may see as 'miracles.' These beings can appear to be physical, but you rarely can see them. It is more likely that you might be able to sense them in other ways.

The Golloids are beings that assist the Mantis and are much shorter and not so thin like the Mantis. These beings are less than six feet tall, are thin, and have brownish-grey skin. They are bipedal and resemble a human in some ways. Their eyes are much larger, but their head is approximately the same size as a human. These beings live for many thousands of years and have shape-shifting abilities. They can move from one dimension to another

Chapter 6 - The Angelic Realm

with ease. Each time they shift from one dimension to another, they take on the physical appearance of the average being in the dimension to which they are shifting. These are also very helpful healing beings, and they work alongside the more advanced Mantis.

Another group in the angelic realm is the Arcturians. They are one of the most advanced spiritual groups that can interact with humankind, but they choose not to interfere. Arcturians can live in many dimensions as they are inter-dimensional, but they originated in the Angelic Realm.

The energy of the 7th, 8th and 9th dimensions—the three dimensions of the Angelic Realm—is completely different. So many distinctions are quite difficult to put into words. Besides energetic, vibrational, and sound differences, the beings that exist in each level vary widely.

Music in the Angelic Realm is extremely important to the Universe. We rarely hear the sounds of angels, but we are more likely to hear angels than see them. They are of such high vibration that when a person experiences the angelic realm, there is instant healing that occurs. During my near-death experience, I found the 7th dimension overwhelming with humming and tones that I would never hear. If I had been in the 7th dimension, I must have forgotten what some of these sounds were, because they felt foreign to me. I understood the gist of the music that I was hearing, and I intend to create the music that I hope will touch the hearts of others. I believe that music is a very strong part of the Angelic Realm, because sound is energy, and the Angelic Realm deepens your personal relationship with the divine. The music should help a person attain better human relationships and help a person perfect their self-expression. This can help produce positive transformation in their daily lives.

Chapter 7 - The Macroscopic Realm

The Macroscopic Realm is comprised of the 10th, 11th and 12th dimensions. The Macroscopic Realm deals with the largest view of our Universe. It is here that one finds the, which stores all the information from all the dimensions. It is also here that spirits would have access to this information, and where creator beings reside. The 10th dimension is where spirits can study the entire Universe and consider the specifics of their involvement.

In the 11th dimension, there are creator beings that work with creating what will be found on planets. Spirits go here to become co-creators of various life forms on planets. In the 12th dimension, there are creator beings who work with our Universal Creator to make planets, stars, and galaxies. Here, spirits become co-creators of stars, galaxies, and planets.

Spirits go to the Macroscopic Realm to access information other spirits have already gathered. It includes the Akashic records, which is a repository for the experiences of every spirit from every planet, in every dimension. There are trillions of different species on trillions of different planets, and all of these experiences are recorded and collected in the Macroscopic Realm. The Akashic records is an energetic library found in the 10th dimension and is accessible from any of the macroscopic dimensions.

The Tenth Dimension

The creator beings have made it easy for spirits to navigate the enormity of the 10th dimension. A spirit may remain stationary and use pure thought to bring the information from the Akashic records into its essence. This is much different than we are used to, where we must hunt down the information from a multitude of resources. In the 10th dimension, it is possible for a spirit to replay an experience that another spirit had during its own incarnation, regardless of species. The Akashic records are much larger than a library on Earth. The library can perform extremely advanced tasks. For example, it is possible to emulate the experience of an eagle flying over the Earth; a spirit would be able to see as the eagle sees and feel the experience as though it were the eagle, because the soul of every being is recording the spirits experiences and transmitting them to the Akashic records. You might have the same experience that another species had during their incarnation.

There is no bit of information that is unimportant to the soul. Spirits have access to the prior experiences of every species that has ever existed on any planet. One might wonder why spirits would choose to incarnate at all when they can have such realistic experiences in the 10th dimension by replaying the experiences of past beings. This is because the 10th dimension does not create new experiences, but rather accesses what has already been experienced through the Infinite Mind, a storage place of all knowledge of all the species of all the planets in the Universes. The Infinite Mind is also referred to as the mind of the Universal Creator. Spirits choose to have new experiences on their own. It is like asking, why would anyone write a new piece of music when someone else has already written music? Spirits desire to create their own experiences, and many of these experiences are unique from one another.

At some point, one would think that many of the experiences would become repetitive, but this is not so. The Universes are all about unlimited possibilities. The possibilities have no beginning and no end. Like a song, they may have a similar beat, but each life still has a different resonance or vibration. Many spirits stay in the 10th dimension for long periods.

A spirit can choose to incarnate onto any planet. The spirit often will choose to return to the same planet for various reasons. Societies are evolving so rapidly that each lifetime provides an entirely new experience. There are billions of people inhabiting Earth, and each one of them is having a vastly different experience despite existing at the same time. How can this be so? Every being is uniquely created, and we are not gifted with the ability to completely understand the perspective of another. Just as there are billions of people, there are also billions of perspectives. Every species has unique perspectives from one another. For example, the life of a raccoon is much different from the life of a starfish. In addition, the life of a starfish in its natural environment is much different from the life of a starfish in an aquarium.

The 10th dimension consists of seven distinct levels.

Level 1: Cartuse

The first level in the 10th dimension is Cartuse. This translates from Romanian to mean *"the cartridges."* Just as if a cartridge is the container for something else, this level contains the information and vast possibilities that lie in the 10th dimension. Cartuse is an introduction, where spirits are shown specifics about how our Universe works. When spirits first reach this level, guides will instruct them about the levels that they will encounter in the Macroscopic Realm. In addition, it is here that we learn about how our energetic bodies work. It is fair to call this a science lesson on spirituality.

Chapter 7 - The Macroscopic Realm

The 10th dimension is teeming with life and most of the life is in the Cartuse level. One would think the 10th dimension is an extremely high point in evolution where there would be limited visitations, but this is not the case. Some spirits spend a lot of time here, but others will vacate it rather quickly to work in other levels once they have the basic understanding of what the 10th dimension is.

Level 2: Chanchic

Chanchic is the second level a place where spirits begin the process of researching the contents of the Akashic records. There is little socialization in Chanchic. Each spirit acts individually and is occupied in its own thoughts. There is a lot to learn in this level, so spirits spend more time here than in Cartuse. Spirits search for a way to create the format for their next new incarnation, and what better way to do that than to review things beforehand. It is like scanning the pages of a menu at a restaurant where one may consider several before selecting the item that would provide just the right dining experience. Any experience will satiate the spirit, but the spirit can only choose one. Once it chooses the experience, it can move to the next level called Fortress.

Level 3: Fortress

At the Fortress level, the spirit samples an experience. If it feels that the experience is going to be valuable, it may choose to incarnate into the corresponding dimension. It can choose to move to any dimension that it wishes. If a spirit feels that it has completed an experience in one dimension, it may move to a new dimension that it has chosen. A spirit also has the option to choose a different experience, but once it is done sampling its choice it will move to the next level or back to Fortress to look at other options.

Level 4: Initiates

The next level is Initiates. In this level, a group of elder spirits, called the *Initiates*, will assist a spirit in choosing a specific personality for its next incarnation. For example, the Initiates may help the spirit decide what dimension to incarnate. They will narrow it down to a particular region in the Universe and to a particular species or race. A spirit may choose to incarnate with a specific soul family, or it may choose a completely new soul family. To review a soul group is like one cluster of grapes of a grape vine and a soul family is like an entire branch of a grape vine. There could be up to two hundred souls in a soul group and billions in a soul family: ex. the human race on Earth. The Initiates assist the spirit by analyzing the soul's past experiences to help the spirit select specific details for the next incarnation.

Level 5: Ascended Masters

In the fifth level, spirits meet with a group of elders and master teachers called the Ascended Masters who give us instructions on the best way to achieve their soul's desires in the next incarnation. They also help spirits choose their Father guide, which is usually someone from its soul family. The Ascended Masters know more than anyone who will make the best father guide for the spirit to ensure the soul needs is met. At this point your father guide communicates with the angelic realm, and you'll be assigned angels for your journey. The father guide communicates to other spirits who may also be guides during the new incarnation. These guides may come and go but your father guide agrees to stay with you for the interim of your incarnation. This guide is usually called the father guide, though this has nothing to do with gender.

Level 6: Comprehension

The Ascended Master will chaperone your spirit through the next level Comprehension. At this level, you will be able to comprehend what your experience will be, by comparing what other spirits' have experienced in similar lives. If deemed important to your soul's goals, you would choose exactly what profession you would like to get into if you are choosing the human experience. Of course, this is not important to a snail or a turtle but it is a good example of refined the process can become. When the spirit incarnates a lot of this information is lost, but in some instances, it will be brought forward to the conscious mind.

Often, the spirit will be given just the right teacher during the incarnation that will help steer a person in the right direction. When the spirit is lost, it can ask for directions, and the angels will put people in our path to assist the spirit. Although angels collaborate well with Ascended Masters, they are not the same thing. The Ascended Masters act as guidance counselors before you incarnate. After you incarnate, you will be working with guides and angels.

Angels work with animals and plants but the Ascended Masters for level six Comprehension are called the overriding Devas. Devas work like the Ascended Masters, but each species of plant and animal will have a different group of Devas. Devas work at balancing nature and bringing about harmony among the food chain. The food chain is important in perpetuating the species.

Level 7: Rest

The seventh level is called the *Rest* level. Spirits are given time to wait for the incarnation to occur. Here the spirit will determine how much energy it will need to complete its incarnation. The Universal Creator supplies the energy, and the spirit will not ask for more energy than it needs to complete its incarnation. It is also in this phase that it will decide its approximate life span for its incarnation. When the desired physical body becomes available to incarnate into, then the spirit will leave the Rest level. The moment that a spirit enters a life form varies greatly. Some spirits enter at a very early point, while others wait until just before birth. This is true for animals as well but for plants, the spirit will enter when the seed sprouts.

The Eleventh Dimension

The 11th dimension is a place where spirits go to become co-creators. They will work under the guidance of its Universal Creator. All spirits helped create something that exists on a planet unless the soul is a new soul. As co-creator's spirits often work in teams, of from two to twelve spirits working on the same creation. Sometimes a project can take a great deal of time to complete.

Many new creations on this Earth are new experiments that are in the experimental stages especially in the insect kingdom. It is easy to see why so many do not flourish for long periods. Most life forms were created on other planets and have been seeded here. Spirits has created all plants and animals in the 11th dimension. These creations are transported to planets by a variety of means.

There are people that commonly report a fondness for a particular plant or animal. Such a person in spirit may have been involved in the creation such as a plant or animal, and some memory of that creation may have been retained and manifest as a fondness. A thought of that plant or animal may recall the spiritual creation experience and trigger a great feeling of love or joy.

The Twelfth Dimension

The 12th dimensional beings assist the Universal Creator to create the planets, stars, and galaxies in our Universe. This is a more complex process. Some galaxies such as the Milky Way that we live in are still growing. Every few thousand years a new planet or solar system may be set into motion. Many spirits have spent only a short amount of time experiencing the 12th dimension, but most spirits spend most of their time in their preferred dimension.

The spirits who visit the 12th dimension who assist in the creation of planets and solar systems do not become Universal Creators themselves. They are merely helpers of the Universal Creator. As described in Chapter 1, the Universal Creators themselves have been created by the Master Creator that is sometimes known and referred to as the source of all. The spirit world calls this source the Master Creator. There is only one Master Creator, which is commonly referred to on Earth as God.

Chapter 8 – The Microscopic Realm

The 13th dimension is known as the Microscopic Realm, but it does not mean just microscopic images, but it is more of an energetic realm. It could be called the energetic realm, but it comprises all the things that the Universe is made of. One could say that the energy below the level of our microscopic capabilities is the 13th dimension. Unlike the other realms that have three dimensions, this realm has only one dimension, although it could be broken down into several units. These units are so difficult to differentiate that for the purposes of this writing, it would be referred to as the 13th dimension only. Eventually, a 14th and 15th dimension will be added to the Microscopic Realm, but this could be billions of years from now.

When one thinks of the term Microscopic Realm, it immediately recalls the use of microscopes. While scientists have discovered that matter is composed of atoms, and even smaller subatomic particles such as quarks. Most energy cannot be seen even with in a microscope. This is because the energy that exists in the 13th dimension, a realm that we can't peer into with our physical three-dimensional eyes. It is the same as not being Just as our eyes are not able to see into the 5th dimension or into the angelic realm. As physical beings, we just do not have the ability to see clearly into these realms beyond the 3rd dimension.

As we have discussed on the Circle of Life diagram, a spirit can choose to incarnate into any dimension at any time. In fact, some new spirits select the 13th dimension as the first one to experience. Beginning one's journey in the 13th dimension provides a unique perspective of the circle of life.

One thing that we have learned in science is that energy can change form but cannot be created or destroyed. This is true, and it should be stressed that even though humans are not capable of destroying energy they can only change the form.

Without the existence of the 13th dimension, none of the other dimensions could exist. Really, the energy of the 13th dimension provided the building blocks on which the Universe was built. Since the Universe was created by thought, then thought is the substances that create the energy which create the 13th dimension. Thirteen different units of energy go into a single atom. There are no microscopes that are capable of peering into the 13th dimension, but if one could, it would reveal the thirteen distinct types of energies that are circulating in a single atom. This has nothing to do with the unit we call an electron, but within an electron, exists the thought that created it.

There have been many experiments in which the nucleus has been removed from a cell and the cell continued to live. In fact, each of our red blood cells loses its nucleus as it matures then goes on to live its entire functional life (over 100 days) without a nucleus. At one time, it was believed that the nucleus was the brain of the cell, but now scientists understand that the nucleus is more like a blueprint. What keeps the cell living is the energy of the 13th dimension.

The Macroscopic Realm was responsible for creating the Microscopic Realm. One would be curious to know what came first in this case, which realm is the chicken, and which is the egg. According to the spirit world, the Macroscopic Realm was created first by thought which itself gave rise to the energy that created the microscopic realm.

We call the 13th dimension the Microscopic Realm referring to its vital energy and other aspects of the complete Universe that exist below our level of understanding. It could have been called the *energetic realm,* for that is what advanced beings refer to when they speak of it.

Chapter 9 – The Circle of Life

The planets are round, the Sun is round, the solar system is round—you may have noticed a recurring pattern in the universal scheme of things. All things in life, electrons, protons, neutrons, quarks, and even the infinitesimal particles are round. That is why the guides say, in the higher order of things, the Universe is round. I was glad to hear it was not square, or worse yet rectangular. Even the concept of infinity implies that things are circular in nature, with no beginning and no end. The completion of your life, therefore, is not its finality but the start of something new, as all things have circularity.

The fact that the solar system appears to be elliptical is the best definition of illusion that we can think of. The Milky Way galaxy also only appears to be nearly linear or elliptical in nature, which is another good example of illusion. Note that the Milky Way has a linear appearance in the sky, and yet it too is circular. This is a hard concept to grasp, so I understand those of you that are having a challenge with this. For example, a cross section of an orange is still round, but when viewed from the side it does not appear to be round. Just remember that your eyes are anything but perfect. When you look in the sky, you are only getting a 2D, flattened perspective and it is completely distorted. It's like your view on life, if you catch my drift.

Many spirits have experienced existences as plants, insects, animals, and other extra-terrestrial life forms as part of this circle of life. The circle of life takes us higher and higher until we reach the vibration that the Universal Creator has prepared for us. Then we exist in a circular spiral fashion to assist all beings on all different dimensions. When you put all the dimensions together, they form a circle. This spiral is also representative of the DNA strands in our genetic make-up. The double helix, as it has been named, is the universal symbol of continuing life. Our extra-terrestrial visitors have been teaching us about humanity and about the circle of life using universally recognizable symbols. These symbols have been imprinted into our "knowing" and are sometimes given to us in the form of crop circles. These crop circles may trigger many forgotten memories in our circle of life and may be used to activate additional strands of our DNA. When these additional strands of DNA become activated, our awareness of the circle of life will increase.

Messages from the Spirit World

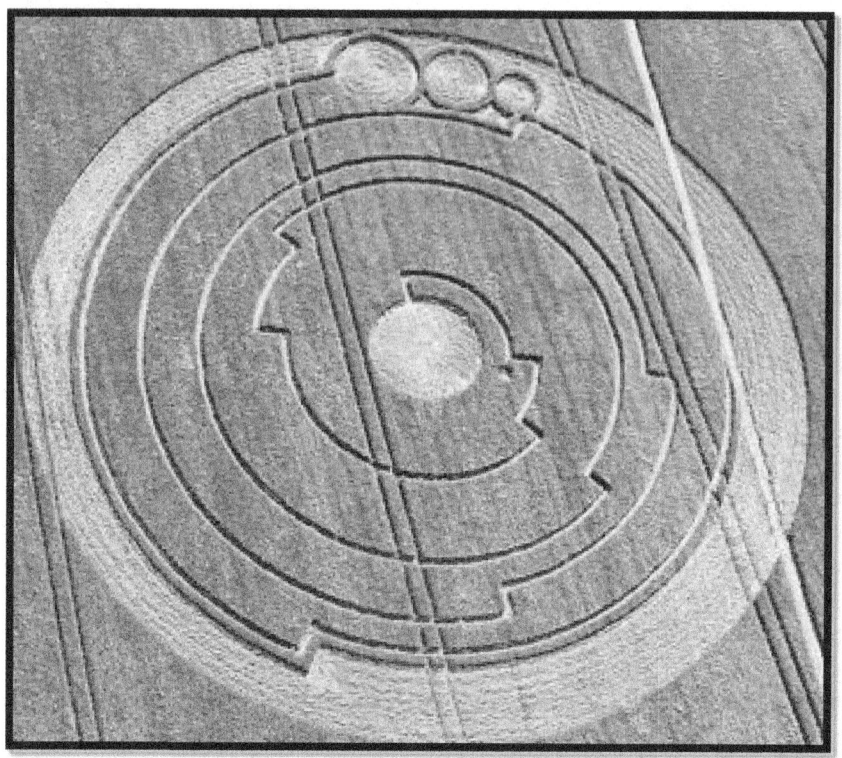

This crop circle, for example, represents the number, Pi. This was an attempt from extra-terrestrials to communicate with humans using mathematics. Pi is used in the mathematical equation to calculate the circumference of a circle. According to the spirit world Pi is also the mathematical number used to represent the Earth.

Our souls incarnate through the circle of life, level by level, in a circular fashion until they've experienced all thirteen dimensions. Newer souls, after liberation from the 3rd dimension, most often choose to move to the next level, the 4th dimension. Older souls who have already completed the thirteen-dimensional circle of life may choose any dimension for their next incarnation.

Note that it is only spirits—not the planet itself—that is moving toward the 4th dimension. It is nearly impossible for a planet itself to move from the 3rd dimension to the 4th, because to do so, it would have to shift realms. Nor is a planet to separate from its solar system, and for it to shift, the entire solar system would have to as well. Humans are evolving to higher levels of awareness, allowing them to access and use more of their natural spiritual gifts but they are not shifting their consciousness as so many believe. Consciousness is states and awareness have to do with levels. They are two different words and should not be subscribed with the same meaning. Within the states of consciousness, there are many levels of awareness. The awareness of the people living on the planet can shift but not the actual matter.

Humans are not leaving the 3rd dimension outright; they are just tapping into more of their psychic abilities that can reach into higher dimensions. As people evolve, they can access their telepathic, psychic, healing, and manifesting abilities. Likewise, some people believe that it's possible for a spirit to ascend with its physical body to a higher dimension. This has been illustrated most prominently in the Bible, as figures like Jesus, Elijah, and Enoch were said to have ascended out and entered heaven alive, and later to have returned to their physical bodies. However, here is the truth: you don't need a physical body in the 6th dimension, which—as mentioned in the previous chapter—is the place we see as Heaven. As I found out during my afterlife experience, Jesus and some other biblical figures had been physically transferred from one dimension to another via teleportation. The Bible is correct that Jesus and the others ascended with their bodies however simply did not go to 'Heaven,' the 6th dimension as we know it. Rather, the most likely would have ascended to the 5th dimension. Fifth-dimensional beings can have physical bodies or light bodies and have the ability to view the 6th dimension. However, they cannot take their physical bodies into the 6th dimension. You can only recognize the energy of beings; your inner vision fills in the details of how you knew them as they looked in the 3rd dimension.

Why would the Bible be slightly misguiding about this? Well, consider this: we as an advanced society can understand concepts such as *dimensions* and *realms* mean. When the Bible was written, many of these concepts and understandings simply did not exist. With current terminology, we can explain more accurately, what the spiritual world is. So, the Bible—and many other ancient spiritual sources like the Talmud and the Torah—do speak to these fundamental truths, albeit in appropriately-ancient terminology.

Interestingly, ancient documents have spoken not only about the truth behind your spiritual existence and other dimensions but have also mentioned extra-terrestrial beings from within your own dimension. Most of these documents originally rested in the ancient Library of Alexandria before it burned. What documents survived, the Catholic Church in Rome has hidden away; in particular, church leaders hid documents about people having ascended into fiery chariots. These, in today's language, would be considered abduction experiences. Besides the Church not being able to explain extra-terrestrial intervention, it was also threatened of losing authority over the people. The religious leaders felt that these writings from the Ancient Library of Alexandria should not be made public.

Before the Library of Alexandria was sacked, another group of religious leaders—an order that preceded the secretive society known as Knights Templar, extant around 1100—copied much of the information that was relevant to the formation of our Universe. In those documents, they found information about the circular order of our Universe and other geometric shapes. For example, the triangle or cone, was to be useful for the collection of free energy to power and develop new technologies. Even the shape of the church steeple was no accident. It was meant to pull in the spirit, and since the church is a place of spiritual enlightenment, this shape was adopted and continues to this day. Had this secretive society not been able to examine those documents, the organization known as the Freemasons, the architects of most of Europe's cathedrals may have never been established.

The predecessors of the Knights Templar wanted to safeguard the information about the spiritual world, away from the hands of the powerful elite. They wanted to use the information for their own good, to break away from the slavery inherent in the governments of the time. They believed they could use the information that came from the esoteric teachings of Christ to become more spiritual and more masterful. Some of these teachings had explained the manner and order of the Universe.

It was believed that this information did not belong in the hands of the common, ordinary man, but in the hands of the learned. The Bible refers to Jesus saying, "You can move a mountain with your mind. You can walk on water." In addition, many other things that we would consider miracles today were in his esoteric teachings. The teachings of Jesus explained that we were in a solar system, and that the Earth revolved around the Sun. He also taught that we were all once a part of God, and that we too could become creators. What Jesus was talking about here, of course, was the 12th dimension—the dimension where the Universal Creators function. There also were many references to reincarnation in his teachings. Most references about reincarnation and extra-terrestrials were kept out of the current Bible. However, there are a few teachings about extra-terrestrials that can be found in the Books of Ezekiel and Psalms.

Chapter 9 – The Circle of Life

We must get back to the topic of the Circle of Life. As humankind evolves to use more of their natural spiritual abilities, there is an order of development. We will first develop "clairaudience," the ability to hear beings from other dimensions. When humankind evolves into the next phase it will develop its ability of "clairvoyance," the ability to visualize messages from other dimensions. The last phase will be "clairsentience," the ability to feel messages from other dimensions.

Many beings in other dimensions of the circle of life have highly developed spiritual abilities. Some of these races are thousands, perhaps millions of years more advanced than those in the 3rd dimension. We would expect them to look different than we do and to have many advanced understandings to offer us.

There are many extra-terrestrial or advanced beings that reside in the 5th dimension. Some look very humanoid, and others appear completely different. They are so far removed from our three-dimensional reality that the only way we could possibly communicate with them is if they would be willing to step down into the three-dimensional world. This rarely happens. However, third-dimensional extra-terrestrials have been involved in our Earth civilization for thousands of years. They mentioned in the writings of ancient civilizations such as Sumerian, Greek, and Egyptian. Most of these third-dimensional extra-terrestrial races have brought teachings to help humanity progress.

Chapter 10 – Science and Spirituality

The information from my spirit guides has remained constant throughout the years. The information from the scientific community, on the other hand, has constantly changed. This is largely because the spirit guides know much more about the function of the Universe than scientists.

Your knowledge about the microscopic world has increased greatly in the last forty years. You live during a technological revolution, but your true nature remains a major issue in academic circles. It is frustrating to see so many people know so little truth. Yet what I learned early in my life is now making headway into scientific communities.

When I was a college student, my professor, Don Myrold, recognized my grades were far above normal. This raised havoc with his curve grading system. This curve rated a person with the highest score as an A. Ten points below the highest score was a B, the next ten points below that would receive a C, and so on. When my professor noticed that I was consistently getting a perfect score, and that the other student's highest scores started at just seventy percent, he called me into his office for a chat. He said he purposely made his exams difficult to make his students study hard. I was the first student to get a perfect score in three different classes. To my surprise, this had never happened before. I was killing the curve, so just to be fair he decided not to include me in the grading. He then offered me a position as his teacher's assistant, which I accepted. The more we grew to know each other, the more he seemed to like me. He invited me once to gathering with a group of his peers; they turned out to be some of the most advanced college professors across the United States. These professors were studying paranormal things that he said the world was not ready to believe.

His group wanted to keep the information secretive, because they did not want to be accused of practicing occult or witchcraft. Coincidentally, the term "occult" is translated as hidden. The meaning of this term has changed to be devil worship. Occult knowledge is certainly not devil worship—or the worship of any deity, for that matter.

There is a long tradition of hermetic and occult knowledge being taught by secretive societies in all the countries of the world. From Ancient Egyptians and Eastern mystics to the Knights Templar and modern times, this is taught and studied at great length. Today, Freemasons are an organized society that carries out wisdom passed down throughout the generations. I even wonder today if in fact my professor was a Freemason. He never admitted that he belonged to any such group.

In my first meeting, I learned that his colleagues were studying the art of astral travel. I had never heard of conscious astral travel, but of course, I knew that when we sleep, we often leave the body. After the gathering, my professor and I had numerous conversations about my experiences in the afterlife. I talked about the dimensions of the Universe and the purpose of incarnating on Earth. Don told me about his own afterlife experiences. I was surprised to find out our experiences were similar. After we learned this about each other, we were able to communicate freely with one another.

It was good to have someone to talk to about these issues. I was not spiritually forthcoming to my peers, and he affirmed that this was for the best, that present-day society would not be anxious to embrace me. He did prophesize, however, that sometime around the year 2000, there would be a giant boom in technology, and that this would help us. He felt that science would advance so drastically that the world would forever change.

At that time, I was asked to join their group. I ignored the offer because I believed that this knowledge should be openly shared. I did not want to be a part of secrecy. If we continue down the pathway of secrecy, I felt we would not advance in our conscious awareness.

He further theorized that time was irrelevant. In his afterlife experience, he saw that soon in our country, we would be able to buy and sell things without even having to go to a store. All we had to do was punch in some numbers on a computer and the items would ship right to our home. It seemed a little far-fetched to me at the time, but I was attentive and fascinated by this information.

When I think back to those days, I recall that every one of his prophecies came true. Don even predicted cell phones; he claimed that people around the world would be able to communicate with one another via a mass communication system. He felt humankind would eventually be able to iron out their differences. He went so far as to predict that governments would still be at war with one another because of their political ideological differences, even though people of different countries would understand one another. My professor believed that this would be the start a new information exchange, and that it would originate in the United States. Eventually he said it could spread throughout the free world.

Today we are experiencing this change in communication via the Internet, which is something I wasn't even sure I would see in my lifetime. My professor suggested that the ones in possession of occult knowledge would have two choices: keep quiet or be targeted for assassination by religious and political factions. It was another good reason that these people were meeting in private.

Don understood why I did not care to talk about my afterlife experience, but he fully expected me to reveal my experiences when the time was right. Since I was young then, I was not willing to take chances with my life, so I kept quiet for many years.

Then I saw how misinformed that the population is about spirituality. The more I saw, I became concerned. No one seemed interested in spirituality. The technology revolution had begun. However, what if we were like young boys playing with matches? Society had advanced in technologically to the point where we might be our own worst enemies. Seeing this, I felt that spirituality had been outstripped by technology, and I thought it was a good time to write my book.

Once the book had been completed, I did a short YouTube video and was able to get someone to help me build an internet website. It was time to spread the word through social media.

This was my first experience with social media. For the most part people were quite complimentary, but a few scoffed. It left me wondering: were they still not ready to hear this? I felt rejected and disheartened. However, the spirit guides explained to me that some people have been indoctrinated with mainstream understandings. They tend only to believe what science can prove. They are not bad people, but just closed in their thinking. Throughout the years, scientists never have agreed with new information, so it is normal that many will reject it at first. It just doesn't go along with what they have been taught. Those who think outside of the box are always the subject of ridicule by religious and scientific thinkers.

Religious thinkers believe that if it is not in the Bible, it simply cannot be true. People who are students of the scientific principles believe that if it is not on Wikipedia, then there is no validity.

The group of thinkers that seems to be most accepting of the information about the spiritual world is quantum researchers. Some of the field's most advanced thinkers say that they are just starting to prove that there are other dimensions. They tend to agree with the models that my guides have presented.

Curiously, mainstream and other religious societies tend to think that guides do not exist. Yet they believe in angels. I find this interesting. I have discussed this to no avail with skeptics. I simply do not understand why a person could believe in the possibility of other dimensions but not in the possibility of entities living in those dimensions. Why is this so hard to grasp? Dimensions must be used for something I conjectured. I have been in contact with spirit guides since a young age, but some skeptics seem to get angry when they hear this. Skeptics doubt the fact that I had a near-death experience and are quite forthcoming with their negative feedback.

In recent years, I have met many people who claim to have had near-death experiences. They all report the same general information. The first common theme: there is an afterlife. Secondly, spirits do exist. There is no difference with afterlife experiences on these points. Thirdly, most experiencers understand that we go somewhere not of this dimension when we die. Fourth: most believe there is a creator being. I have not heard of a single case where someone has claimed that they have met the creator being—or any creator being for that matter—in an afterlife experience. The fifth significant observation: there exist master teachers and angels. Sixth: we meet relatives or loved ones while in these dimensions. They appear to have been younger than at the point at which they passed away. Lastly, many afterlife experiencers believe they have been to heaven. They speak of a place that is so beautiful, one could not imagine; where pain, agony and emotions do not exist.

What I find to be most fascinating is that none of the afterlife experiencers believe that science has truly developed in its understanding of the Universe. Most believe we are only aware of a miniscule part of scientific truth, and that their own near-death experience has humbled them to that truth.

When I had my aterlife experience, I was shocked to find out how badly I had been lied to by previous generations. I now have come to the realization that these ancestors were misinformed about the truth of the Universe.

In 2014, on a social media site, I noticed a comment from someone regarding a particular fast-food restaurant that was withholding information about what ingredients were in their French fries. I remembered in the 70's, I participated in a research project in Canada. The study was to determine why so many Americans frequently had parasites in their digestive tract. The researchers attempted to discover the source of the parasites. In the 70's, I was having difficulty with my health. The researchers concluded that the microorganisms were present in oil that is used to cook French fries in the fast-food restaurants.

Before this study, people believed that parasites were destroyed during cooking. However, this new information demonstrated that certain parasites could survive temperatures of 375 degrees Fahrenheit. There is a group of parasites called thermophiles, which can survive up to 700 degrees. The researchers attempted to release the information to the public, but United States researchers discredited the results. The Canadian researchers found that if the cooking oil was changed daily, the amount of microbiological growth diminished greatly.

When I posted a comment that many fast-food restaurants could still be propagating the growth of parasites, people started to voice their opinion. These people seemed to think they knew it all, and yet none of them had any formal training in microbiology. When I investigated the profile of the people making the rude comments, I found that they included CEOs, a police officer, and even a janitor. I assume they derived their vast wisdom from a source known as Wikipedia, or something similar that is posted free on the internet. I laughed to myself, because I knew that Wikipedia is only as good as the people who posted the information. The internet is anything but complete when it comes to validity. It is not the final authority, though people are treating Wikipedia as the sacred source of all knowledge.

Even though the comment I made on the social site could be quite useful, the naysayers were determined to win their argument. They insisted on having the last word on the subject. These people were going to do everything in their power to discredit me for speaking my truth, and I was again disheartened. The naysayers presented many shortsighted arguments to prove that everything I said was poppycock. My son suggested that I quit responding to their angry posts. Yet I felt bad people were being lied to by those who do not even have a rudimentary understanding of microbiology.

My guides inform me that there are even political reasons as to why true information is withheld. In the future science will glean new understandings that closely parallel what my spirit guides have been telling me. This is only one good example of how misinformed people can be.

I am hopeful that the public will understand that many of our misconceptions will be laid to rest. I am trying to reach the people that want this information now. I have presented my best understanding about the afterlife, but of course, not all of it will be embraced. At least this information is now available to those who want it.

We can all be a little less condemning to those people that are presenting new information. A little time and research go nowhere if you are drawing your information from a low source such as the bantering of some misinformed social media troll, whose sole purpose is to stir up trouble and create controversy.

As our society advances, so will the understanding that science and spirituality are connected. In time, technology can yet overtake our understanding of the spiritual world. If this occurs, it could be a dangerous world to live in. Now is the time to focus on humankind's spiritual development, before we become a threat to our own existence.

Part 2 – The Structure of the Mind

In this part, I will discuss how the mind is structured. I will also go into detail about the inner workings of the three minds. You can make a vast difference in the world if you first understand how your mind works. How you understand yourself has a lot to do with the inner workings of the mind.

Chapter 11 – Thought Energy

Everything in existence is created and sustained by the energy of thought. Thought transmits energetic intent out into the Universe. This paves the way for actions to occur, which helps orchestrate the manifestation of the thought. Consider the following example to illustrate the concept.

Imagine you have a five-acre plot of land; you could build a house, plant trees, plant a garden and landscape. In addition, while each activity would require plenty of hard labor or money, it all begins with an idea or a thought. To an insect, those five-acres of land literally would be the entire Universe. You would create your own tiny "Universe" where you live, without even knowing it.

Therefore, everything begins with a thought. It was an *'aha moment!'* for me. I hope that this is an *'aha moment'* for you too. That reality hit home so hard that it ran shivers down my spine the first time I heard about it. You were created by thought, and you are here to think and create. Once you think and create, you experience. You came to the Physical Realm to experience. Everything you do extends from thought.

I remembered a course I had taken in college about thinking but had never quite grasped back then. I had read "Think and Grow Rich" by Napoleon Hill, and "The Power of Positive Thinking" by Norman Vincent Peale. Both authors described that what we are thinking creates our own reality. It seems so obvious now I wish I had understood it then.

There is another aspect of thinking that previously I had not quite understood but later understood as the Universe being only what you think it is. It turned out that my understanding was incomplete, and the spirit world corrected me on that one in a hurry. In actuality, the world is more than just what *I* think. It matters greatly what everyone in the Universe thinks. On Earth, if there are enough people thinking similar thoughts, then those thoughts will come to fruition.

So just how powerful are our thoughts alone? Do our thoughts have limits? We used to think that man couldn't fly until the Wright Brothers came along with the invention of the airplane. At one time, it was believed that if a man traveled faster than thirty miles per hour that his body would disintegrate. Now we take supersonic flight and even space travel for granted. In the same way, our understandings should have no limits. Thoughts are a lot more powerful than we allow them to be. Only our belief systems restrict the power of our thoughts. The spiritual teachings of certain Eastern religions have broken though limiting belief resulting in profound discoveries, such as levitation and to travel up to forty feet between footsteps by breaking the gravity bounds. In our Western world, we believe a broken leg will take weeks—if not months—to heal, whereas the aboriginal tribes in Australia (who believe in "dreamtime") believe a broken leg is healed in a few minutes. We would benefit greatly by removing our limited mindset to expand the power of our conscious thoughts. I had an experience once healing a woman's broken leg at a fair many years ago. She had fallen right in front of me. I helped her to a chair and asked if she wanted me to help remove the pain, to which she agreed. We were surprised when within minutes, her leg had stopped hurting completely, and she could walk without pain. Just to be sure, she had x-rays taken of her leg. The doctors were able to see where the leg had broken, but what they found was that it looked like it had occurred some time ago.

In healing others, the spirit world explains that your thoughts are most effective when directed to another person with a specific intent in mind than if they are directed to nowhere specific. If two people are thinking about healing another person who is sick, the effectiveness of their combined thoughts is more than doubled. My spirit guides also told me that there is more power in a prayer or request directed for others than for oneself.

Before I go further, it might interest you to know where your thinking comes from. Your spirit sends out electrical impulses to the neural pathways in the brain to trigger thoughts. The truth is thinking is done with an incredibly small portion of the spirit that lies outside your body. The spirit also sends out electrical connections to all parts of the body, providing the necessary spark to keep your bodies alive. Occasionally, people tell me they feel like they're losing connection with their spirit. They are, because some of these electrical connections have been cut off. You can feel the connections to your spirit; you just can't see them. For example, there is an area right in the center of our heart that would cause us to die if cut during open-heart surgery. This is one of the main energetic pathways that connect you to your spirit.

The spirit mind has three major components; the largest part of the spirit mind is the superconscious. It makes up 88 percent of the total mind. Then there are the conscious and the subconscious minds, which contribute to the remainder about equally. How each component of your spirit mind works to manifest and create your own reality through thoughts and prayers will be discussed in later chapters.

Another concept my spirit guides would like clarified is that of the 'higher self.' The spirit guides do not refer to the superconscious as the *'higher self'*. If you ask your *'higher selves'* to create a manifestation or an intended desire, then you are only using a small part of our superconscious potential. Therefore, I will refer to the superconscious mind, instead of the *'higher.'* In addition, the spirit world does not want you to conclude that there is a *'higher self'* then there must also be a *lower self*. This implication can confuse you and serve to mislead. There is no part of your consciousness that is less important. I've found this to be a source of contention for people who are so engrained in speaking of the *'higher self'* but when one understands how powerful words really can be this ceases to be a source of contention. When you reach the chapter on the superconscious mind, you will learn just how powerful the superconscious really is.

Have you ever noticed that sometimes you seem to sense other people's thoughts or emotions? Have you felt that you're aware of not only yourself, but of the conscious minds around you? That is because conscious thought is distributed all throughout the Universe. Thoughts do not travel only in our three-dimensional world. They also travel in another plane—the spirit world and can even be sent clear across the Universe.

Chapter 12 – The Human Mind and Brain

You might think that the human brain and the human mind are the same. However, this is a widely misunderstood idea. The mind is separate from the brain. As mentioned earlier, the mind resides in your spirit, and the superconscious part of your mind connects electrically to the neural passages in the brain. The brain receives sensory input from your various senses. This information is transmitted to the superconscious mind and from there gets stored in the soul. The brain builds pathways to the sensory information that it has stored in the soul, but it is not responsible for the actual thought processes. What it records is just sensory stimuli and information about the environment that you are experiencing. Many computational processes occur in the brain at one time. Over an hour, as many as 50,000 to 100,000 separate observations are made and recorded by the soul. For example, remembering what you had for breakfast three weeks ago last Sunday may be a difficult feat for your short or long-term memory pathways. However, this does not result in sensory overload when stored in the soul. If the neural pathways of the brain are not functioning properly, the superconscious mind can repair the damage to the brain.

The mind can be compared to the brain, in that the brain acts as a command center for the physical body, and the superconscious mind acts as the command center for the spirit. These command centers are vastly different. The mind command center can trump the reactions of the brain command center. For example, the act of being struck by an external physical object, prompts the brain to act quickly to avoid further confrontation. The brain will feed all the sensory stimuli to the mind so that the mind can make a judgment as to the most appropriate response. This rational response occurs in the mind and not the brain. The brain is only capable of instinctual responses. In this manner, it is easy to see that the mind serves a much higher function. If there is too large a gap in time between the data fed to the mind, regrettable actions can occur. This is a good example of why automatic weapons can be so dangerous. Most regrettable actions occur because the mind isn't given enough time to process data fed to it by the brain so the brain triggers an immediate impulse reaction. This is a common scenario in self-defense shootings.

Some researchers have coined the phrase '*reactionary mind*.' They believe that as information reaches the brain, the brain automatically responds according to its preprogrammed instinctual tendencies. '*Reactionary mind*' is somewhat of a misnomer, because instinctual responses are direct actions of the brain, and are not processed by the mind. Although animals have spirits, many of their actions are instinctual. Their instincts are directly responding before the stimuli can be objectified by the mind within. This immediate instinctual response is necessary as programmed by the Master Creator for the perpetuation of the species.

We have many instinctual responses to stimuli that are also called urges. For example, the urge for the human male to breed is an instinctual response that can be for many males a nuisance. These urges may be overridden by the mind. Alcohol interferes with the processing of information passed between the brain and the mind. With less higher-level feedback returning from the mind, the brain is left to act more on impulse. This is why inebriated people make poorer decisions, in some cases, with embarrassing or even dire consequences. Many legal and street drugs distort or hide information that the brain would normally send to the mind. This can result in unethical decisions that do not conform to the mind's original intent. It is rare that a mind has malicious intent, but people who are wounded emotionally may make decisions that result in harm to others especially when they are in a drug-induced state.

There is a common saying, "I was not in my right mind when I said that." It would be more technically accurate to say, "I was not *'using'* my mind when I said that."

The mind knows right from wrong, whereas the brain makes no ethical determinations. The brain is simply an intermediary that follows built-in instructions, like instincts, or carries out the instructions set forth from the mind of the spirit. There is another common expression, "If he had half a mind, he would not have done that." This is an interesting expression because it points out the understanding that the mind makes judgments.

Although there are no substantial limits to how much sensory stimuli the brain can process, there are often delays in how fast the brain can sort and convey information to the mind. If too many of the sensory stimuli are negative, and there is too large of a gap between stimuli, then the individual can become incensed or angered as a part of the normal instinctual process. Others will view these people as being temperamental. Temperamental individuals sometimes inadvertently store up or hide sensory inputs for processing later. Too much stored up sensory stimuli, if negative, can cause an outburst referred to as a temper tantrum when described in children. Such individuals, as they mature, are sometimes labeled as being hotheaded or imbalanced. Although other conditions can exaggerate the imbalance, much of the display of temper is controllable but the individual needs to allow

Chapter 12 – The Human Mind and Brain

more time for sensory processing before acting. The 'let me think about this' attitude is an effective mental approach to staving off the instinctual responses.

It is also important to remember that we can regulate our emotions. When receiving negative sensory stimulus, we have the choice of how we want to react. For example, the act of someone spilling milk, should not elicit anything but an apology, and we should view it as a rather humorous incident of one's own clumsiness. It is irrational for the mind to expect perfection, even though some anger may trickle in.

At times, the human brain can make errors, but we should be viewing these things as a method of learning. Many times, loading one down with too many thoughts or responsibilities can result in mistakes or errors that result from the lack of judgment. For example, attempting to do multiple tasks that require our primary attention could result in an accident. Texting while driving an automobile is a good example of an accident that can occur from this lack of judgment. For a person to maintain proper communication between the brain and the mind, we should focus on one task at a time.

Our body has a method of healing and keeping us focused. This healing occurs on a subconscious level while we sleep. Sleep restores the electrical pathways and improves communication between the brain and the mind. Our efficiency depends upon the quality and duration of our sleep. Although the duration of sleep varies, the primary sleep patterns are instinctual. The best time to begin sleep starts at sunset and ends at sunrise. This is more difficult in regions that have short periods of darkness, such as Alaska during the summer, as the body must fight its own natural instincts. Ideally, we would work most efficiently if we lived in places that provided us with at least six to seven hours of darkness.

We have all heard of false prophets. These people use others for their own agenda. Greedy individuals who are well to do and seek positions in society of power and influence are often misleading. They are employing the use of mind control and another term for it is black magic. It is important to understand how subjected to mind control we are and may not even be aware of it. Television is a form of mind control and not just the advertisers use it. The television news is loaded with mind control. The people who control the television networks know how much power they have over us and can keep us glued to the television by activating the part of our brain that absorbs stimuli. Those spreading the agenda of the world leaders may not realize they are contributing to mind control. False prophets seem to be lacking joy in their lives, and as a result they may suffer from lack of love. The love they tend to receive is often quite phony and illusionary.

There are many religious and political leaders that use mind control through their intentions may differ. How do we stop it? The spirit world suggests sending prayers or positive intentions to these leaders so that they modify their attitudes. There are endless possibilities of other remedies; this may just be one of the best and easiest remedies to employ.

In addition, we can meet unscrupulous individuals in the astral plane or what is also known as the 4th dimension and embrace them with love and positive intention. There is an enormous number of activities taking place in the 4th dimension.

Many refer to travel in the astral body as an out-of-body experience. It is much easier to reason with a troubled soul in the 4th dimension than the 3rd dimension because of the absence of limiting factors of the conscious mind. In the 4th dimension mind control has no power.

The conscious mind can get confused if parts of itself are left behind. There is a strong belief that the soul leaves energy fragmentations behind. This can occur because of physical injury, or emotionally hurtful events. These energy fragments serve as a way to shed off unwanted experiences for a period but leave the soul with less of its energy. Really, the soul does not lose its energy, but the spirit does. Some individuals practice the art of "soul recovery" for the express purpose of repairing individuals who appear to be lost or confused. They may call it "soul recovery" but since the soul is incapable of being damaged, they are really referring to the energy that the spirit has left behind. Perhaps it should be called "spirit recovery." Spirit recovery works by returning energy fragments to the spirit and in turn, that rejuvenates the soul. Spirit recovery is good for the mind, therefore.

Chapter 13 – The Three Minds

We have been told that our minds are more powerful than we give credit for. In reality, this is because we actually have three minds. Most of the information that I have read includes little about the superconscious mind, but it has a lot to say about the conscious and subconscious mind. This something I would like to explain more in depth. My spirit guides have been telling me for most of my life that we have given credit to the subconscious mind for powers that the superconscious mind possesses. If we could see how limited the scopes of the conscious and subconscious minds are, we would take our focus in another direction. Understanding the superconscious mind strengthens our ability to manifest and creates a healthier environment for our personality and spirit to communicate.

One of the first things my guides ask me to tell my clients is the fact that we have three minds. Nobody seems too surprised, because intuitively we recognize that. We know many things intuitively, but that does not mean we are always willing to follow our intuition. Learning about understanding the three minds is a step in the right direction for people who are eager to strengthen their abilities to heal themselves. Although this process of self-healing might take longer than through a trained healer, it can be just as effective. There are many Biblical teachings in the New Testament that aim to make us understand that we are all healers. There are many references to miracles, and those miracles had to do with healing. Miracles depend upon the power of the superconscious mind. At the time however, the teachers did not have the precise terminology to describe it.

It comes as no surprise that Jesus taught us about the spiritual realm. However, we may forget that Jesus had to use terminology of the times to refer to celestial concepts. Our society has completely misunderstood his lesson on the Trinity: the Father, the Son, and the Holy Ghost. The common interpretation of this is that Jesus was referring to the celestial hierarchy. Although this is partly correct, the truth is much deeper. The Master Creator is indeed the "Father," but the Universal Creator, not Jesus himself, is the "Son." Moreover, your spirit is the "Holy Ghost." However, the Master Creator has also set up within each of us another trinity; that of the three minds.

Your 'mind'—the part of you that thinks, understands and interprets—is made up of three separate components, each that correlate to one part of Jesus' trinity. The "Father" of your minds is the superconscious mind, the

"Son" is the subconscious mind, and the "Holy Ghost" is the conscious mind.

Each of the three minds is discussed in more detail in the later chapters. Broadly defined, the three minds are the:

- **Conscious Mind** – which interacts with the physical realm.
- **Superconscious Mind** – which interacts with the spiritual realm.
- **Subconscious Mind** – which stores experiences and memories.

Chapter 14 – The Conscious Mind

It's easy to assume that we know a lot about the conscious mind. Many believe it's simply the part of us that is *aware*; for example, what we see, think, and feel. The conscious mind has more functions than just perceiving the world through our senses; it also has a lot to do with your personality. However, it's important to recognize that the conscious mind is not the totality of one's overall existence, it is only one component. Everything that occurs in the conscious mind transmits to the superconscious mind and is relayed to the soul. Some data is sent to the subconscious mind. The focus of the conscious mind is to operate within the physical environment, whereas the focus of the superconscious mind is to perpetuate knowledge and wisdom. Our soul's personality is a collection of experiences accumulated from our souls previous incarnations whereas our personality is mostly from the experiences within the current lifetime. The things we might be attracted to can be a strong reflection of the soul's personality.

The conscious mind is capable of different 'states.' In each of these states, our conscious mind connects to the world differently. As we will see in the following definitions of states, we can be operating from different states of our conscious mind simultaneously, but most people work predominantly in only one state at a time. We can also shift to different states of mind as we grow and expand our consciousness. It is important that we be able to experience different states of mind, as each state is uniquely suited to dealing with different types of life's challenges. For example, being in *suneidesis* is perfect for an entrepreneur to generate new business ideas; however, the same entrepreneur needs to get to the *noetic* state of mind to market those ideas effectively to investors or potential customers.

By learning about these seven states, we will be able to better understand how we—and everyone around us—is mentally processing the data in the world. We will be able to identify what state of conscious mind those around we are in, and in doing so, we will be better equipped to empathize and communicate.

Conscious State I - Suneidesis

The first state of our conscious mind is *suneidesis* (sun-ee-deh-sus). In this state of mind, our thought processes can be erratic and scattered, changing rapidly. *I like bananas. Wow look at that bus! Did I remember to take out the trash? God my head hurts!* Approximately every second a new thought may interject making it difficult to stay on topic. Does this sound familiar? In this state of mind, we find it difficult to follow through on your decisions. Before any decisions are made, new ideas interject and distractions can derail the decision-making process.

Others can heavily influence us when we are in a suneidesis state, which may cause us to be swayed by ideas that conflict with our own values. People in the suneidesis state should be especially wary of those with hidden agendas. For example, we may be working toward creating a healthier lifestyle for yourself by eating at home where we can prepare our own meals. Yet a friend invites us to go out to a restaurant, maybe because we always pay, and again we end up paying. We may even order the rich dessert afterwards. Here is another example: we might find that we know we need to be somewhere at 9:00 am, but we end up jumping on our computer on the way out and get caught up answering emails, which causes us to show up late.

Though the suneidesis state tends to make people seem flighty or distracted, this is not an entirely problematic state and is appropriate for particular situations. For instance, children frequently stay in this state of mind. Suneidesis is the primer for finding new ideas and solving problems. As long as people do not remain stuck in this state, suneidesis can help them to grow. It is a perfect state for brainstorming when beginning a project. One can come up with all sorts of ideas without committing to any one. The mind's natural filters and critiques are pushed aside and permitting us to come up with many thoughts at will. This state is not by nature a problematic; it only becomes a problem for those who stay in it for a long time, making it hard to act on their ideas and bring them to fruition. As adults, we might get too scattered and distracted, keeping us from taking care of our everyday responsibilities. People stuck in suneidesis usually must rely on family or friends to take over of their responsibilities. They may never achieve their own independence. If we enable someone, we may end up thwarting the progression of their own spirit. As we may remember, one of the spirit's functions is to grow, experience, and enrich itself by living a full life. We can't achieve that if we aren't responsible for our own lives. Some people are so stuck in the state that they ultimately surrender themselves to adult care or their lives completely fall apart.

If we find ourselves unfocused and feel stuck in suneidesis, there's a simple solution to getting to a higher, more-focused state of conscious. We must request that our superconscious move us to a higher state of mind. It will be easy at first to remain distracted, so we must continue to ask our superconscious mind to raise us. It may happen in minutes; it may take months. Nevertheless, if you ask enough, we'll come to find we can focus better, that the mind might not be so flighty. Some people can change their mental state at will and relatively quickly. For example, mothers attending to their children need to filter many thoughts before choosing where to focus. They are quickly migrating from suneidesis to the next level, samone.

Conscious State II – Samone

The second state of the conscious mind is *samone* (sa-moan). In this stage, we find new ideas are processed more thoroughly and with less distraction than in suneidesis. Although one may still come up with new, innovative ideas in samone, each idea will be studied and developed it beyond its initial concept. This is where pure creativity can begin to take shape; where an artist first decides upon what medium they to work in, or where a writer begins writing the story.

In this state of the conscious mind, we can more easily work out difficulties. New thoughts will interject at a much slower pace, roughly one to four minutes apart, compared to the one idea every second in suneidesis. This is an important distinction between samone and suneidesis; though we receive ideas less frequently, we are more likely to identify the better ideas and more carefully develop them. In samone, we tend to be more reflective and meditative. We find it much easier to concentrate; therefore, more ideas that are creative can emerge. People who rely most heavily on samone are creative. They tend to become artists, musicians, politicians, or religious leaders. As a musician and writer, I often am in this state. The writers Wadsworth and Longfellow also remained heavily in samone. Such conscious thinkers find that ideas come quite easily, and that they can influence others with the force of their ideas—when talking to people who are in the suneidesis state of conscious mind.

Just like suneidesis, it is dangerous for a person to stay completely in the samone state. A person stuck in samone will start projects—unlike in suneidesis, where a person is more apt to simply talk about projects, but may abandon each project, or will not complete a project effectively. Entrepreneurs who face financial difficulty may have become stuck in this state by getting their businesses off the ground, but not following through and bringing them to a place of profitability. When we meet someone who is in samone, we can take him or her more seriously than someone in suneidesis, who may have strong passions, but be weak in convictions. We may be able to help a person in samone to move through this state by asking some pointed questions. For example, if someone wants us to invest in their idea, ask them whether they are willing to take it to the next step. Ask them about what their goals are, or what they intend to do next with the project. If they can tell us, in specific detail, what the project will become, they are already beginning to move beyond samone. Don't be afraid if they show plenty of excitement for their project, if they enjoy talking about it enthusiastically; that's just the inspiration of samone. However, know that they can't stay there forever. We can help them along with the process by asking those types of questions. If the strength of their convictions is not enough, it will come through in their answers.

When we find ourselves in samone and feel ready to move on to the next state of consciousness, ask our superconscious mind for assistance. We can even ask the superconscious mind to sharpen your convictions in moving on to the next state of mind. The superconscious mind will know exactly what to do. Remember: we need to be both specific and repetitive when dealing with the superconscious mind. The superconscious mind does not act on half-hearted requests.

Conscious State III – Noetic

Noetic is the third state of the conscious mind. In this, state people are less apt to come up with new ideas and are more apt to engage with the people around them. They tend to speak in a more structured, deliberate manner that is intended to inform.

Public speakers and effective teachers are good examples of noetic-minded people. Noetic thinking helps people to ignore distractions and stay focused on a problem until the most plausible solution has been reached. When in noetic, people are better at making sound decisions than those in the samone state of consciousness. It is possible to solve even the most complex problems in this state of mind. But if we're like most people we will let somebody else do the hard problem solving while we're out basking in the sun on a tropical beach! When we become engaged in reading a book or watching a movie, we are no doubt experiencing the noetic state of consciousness. It's good to change gears occasionally! Being in this state does not make us smarter but it does make us think longer and harder.

After a project is in full swing, we may need to move into the noetic state of mind to bring it to completion. The noetic state will help us to both complete the project and present it to others effectively. However, people in this state may have trouble coming up with new ideas, being so attached to the ideas they have already developed. These people may be considered backseat drivers, pushing people to do what they can't.

If we know someone who seems stuck in this state, first find out whether we can focus their talents. Can they provide us with advice on our own projects? If their talents are being used and tested, they are still growing spiritually. However, it's easy for someone in the noetic state to become complacent. They may think they've done everything their spirit expects of them and may become dejected.

If we think someone's noetic state is detrimental—or if we find ourselves stuck there—consider ways of breaking 'out of the mold.' Exposure to new concepts and challenges, taking up a new sport, travel, or reading books on new subjects can encourage investigation and development of fresh ideas. If you start exploiting beyond the familiar, what you're used to and comfortable with, we'll begin to be inspired—and to inspire those around us.

Conscious State IV – Delusional

The fourth state of the conscious mind is the *delusional* state. Although the name sounds negative, there is nothing inherently wrong with this state. In this context, it means a person is in a daydream of sorts. This is different from suneidesis, as it is focused more on one grandiose idea. For example, we might think we are going to run for President and expect to win even though no one knows whom we are. This isn't an inherently problematic thing; in fact, some of these seemingly delusional concepts—tailored with samone inspiration and noetic sensibilities—can make those crazy dreams come true. If someone doesn't remain in the delusional state, it can propel someone into new, creative aspirations. Fundamentally, the delusional state of mind is simply this: the daydream has become a pipe dream.

It is not always easy to know if someone is operating in the delusional state of mind. Some of these people can be successful because they are not afraid to take chances that a person in samone would never think of taking. In this state, people can become single-minded and cannot be easily distracted, at times to the point of being obsessive. I have met people who find it difficult to think of anything but problem-solving and may even look for problems where none exist. They might have grandiose ideas that may sound quite rational, even to others, but have no basis. Their views of the world can become distorted to the point that they become argumentative with others.

I had a best friend who was in the delusional state of mind. He always talked about working on these big business deals, but he was unable to provide for his own basic needs. In his mind, he was gainfully self-employed, and he thought he was going to become tremendously wealthy. Being in the delusional state of conscious mind does not necessarily mean that a person is delusional in the psychological sense. Instead, someone may simply have difficulty discerning his or her role and may find it difficult to finish a task or a job that needs to be completed. Time bleeds by quickly; hours and even years can pass while someone is engrossed with one problem, one concern.

While most people can simply dip into the delusional state of mind, it can be triggered by an accident or from intense emotional scarring. I had a friend once who went through a painful divorce and could never again get a grip on anything that was real. Researchers have discovered that people with lesions around the brain stem may suffer from disorientation and hallucinations. In severe cases, they may even forget who they are.

When people become intoxicated, they can enter the delusional state of mind. The difference between intoxication and injury is that after the alcohol or drug wears off, a person can return to one of the other states of consciousness. However, if the alcohol or drug does any permanent brain damage, then the conscious mind may not be able to function normally after that. It might be difficult to know in what state of mind such people are. They might be connecting to multiple states at the same time making communication difficult.

If we meet people in the delusional state, it's best not to invest too much money or time in them, but don't assume that they have nothing to teach us. Some of the greatest concepts in the world came from people with delusional ideas; Thomas Edison and Sam Walton both functioned mainly in the delusional state of mind. However, the difference here was that they had money and hired people of other states of mind to build their pipe dreams and bring them into reality. When society first heard about Thomas Edison's ideas, he was dismissed as just a pipe-dreamer. Nevertheless, through work and a balancing of the other states of mind, he was able to produce great things.

False information can lead to delusional ideas. If a person has been taught something erroneous but subconsciously understands it to be true, that information could derail the person's life course. Those who spread false information are false prophets. The spirit world avoids communicating with these people. Most false prophets can be easily identified. They spread rumors that are strictly fear-based whereas true prophets will send messages of hope and inspiration.

Chapter 14 – The Conscious Mind

Conscious State V – Delirium

Just when we thought it couldn't get worse, it can, and I'm here to tell us that no one likes how they feel in the mind state of delirium. People often enter delirium when heavily intoxicated. They become severely disorientated, irrational, and can find it difficult to form clear thoughts.

In this state, people may feel disconnected from their own identities to the point of even not being sure of whom they are. Often, people in delirium are unable to do things like cook or care for themselves. They may seem listless, staring out beyond the horizon or may even seem to be in a vegetative state.

If we know someone the state of delirium, first consider what might be causing this. Chemical imbalances or drugs can similarly put people to fall into the state of delirium. Brain disturbances like strokes can also bring someone into this state. One may also shift into delirium as a consequence of staying too long in the delusional state of mind. Although this is a problematic mind state for the spirit, it remains connected with the body. Even if a person is in a vegetative condition, or the spirit is still half in the body; the spirit only leaves completely at the time of death.

So do not abandon the person in delirium. There's still hope that the body can restore itself to a better conscious state. But don't provide medication if it's a purely spiritual problem—no number of drugs can fix the electrical connections with the spirit. It is solely the individual's responsibility to enter a better conscious state. Unlike other states, one cannot directly help another out of delirium. The body must make the necessary repair.

Conscious State VI – Comatose

The sixth state of the conscious mind is the *comatose* state, in which people appear to be unconscious (not counting regular sleep) for more than six hours. The comatose state of the conscious mind occurs when one is alive, but disconnected from control of the body. Someone in comatose can still think, but has lost the connection from the more direct physical self. The comatose state is a last-ditch effort of sorts; the body is shut down even more than in delirium to heal.

If we are beginning to think that there are multiple bad states of consciousness, we are starting to get the picture. It may be surprising to learn that comatose is part of the *conscious* mind, but it is. In a sense, even this state of mind is good; that is, the Universal Creator programmed us with the ability to save ourselves from losing our bodies to pain or dysfunction. The Universal Creator provided us with comatose for our own protection and preservation.

In comatose, people remain connected with the Universal Creator, and as such, have the ability to process their own thoughts. If this seems unbelievable, consider the many comatose people who have recalled what happened around them during their comas.

In comatose, the person fails to respond to stimuli such as light or sound or sharp pains and has lost control of many bodily functions. This can be caused by a stroke, heart attack, or other debilitating injury to the physical body. During this state, the spirit is more mobile, leaving and returning to the body at different times. The spirit can't stand to sit around; after all, its main purpose is to interact with the world. If we know someone who is in a comatose state, remember this: their spirit will often return to their body when in the presence of another spirit. As such, when we visit the body of someone who is comatose, we are very likely attracting their spirit back into the room. The comatose person will be able to hear us, though will unlikely be able to respond.

Conscious State VII – Afterlife

The seventh state of the conscious mind is when the spirit merges back into the spirit world, leaving only an energetic imprint on Earth. It is known as *'afterlife'*, in which the physical body is disconnected from the spirit. Even in death, one remains conscious; as mentioned, the conscious mind exists outside of the body. Who would ever think that the afterlife is still partly conscious? If we have any belief in ghosts, then we might understand that although these people are passed on they still might have a certain agenda. The conscious state of mind goes on even after the body physically dies.

Because the spirit is conscious while in this part of afterlife, the afterlife is considered one of the conscious states of the mind. It is only when the spirit has completely left the Earth plane, that one is no longer considered to be in a conscious state of mind. After the spirit rejoins the soul and transfers what it has learned to the soul, all that it has experienced and remembered. It ceases to be an independent entity. When one reincarnates, it is actually as a new spirit, thus starting a new cycle of consciousness.

Although most spirits stay briefly in the afterlife ghosts are rare spirits that linger in the afterlife state for long periods. Most hauntings are not true ghosts. They are simply disembodied beings of the 4th dimension that have capabilities of multidimensional tasking.

A ghost is not pushing things off shelves and turning off lights. Rather it is a spark of energy—a spirit—that no longer interacts with physical matter. People may *sense* the presence of another consciousness, but often cannot directly see them. There are, of course, exceptions to this as ghosts sometimes have a visceral appearance.

Most ghosts know that their bodies are gone. They remain in the afterlife state because they are trying to communicate with us. They have moved into the 4th dimension and find it hard to get back to the physical realm. They may have some unfinished business that they are trying to resolve. It might be to right some injustice, be it something that happened to them or something they did. Ghost search for people open to receiving information. There select people who are able to see ghosts in the 3rd dimension but it is rare that they find such gifted individuals. Most of the people who believe in ghosts, or that have been contacted by ghosts can sense their presence but may not be able to see them. In my own experience I cannot see ghosts but my guides tell me where they are at. I have been successful at helping people get the ghosts out of their homes. The spirit guides communicate with them and are responsible for their removal. Remember, if we ever feel that we're in the presence of a ghost—they're not dangerous or mischievous; rather they're trying very hard to communicate.

An Overview

We all experience these seven states of the conscious mind at some points in our lives. Often, these states are intermingling between each other; we may acquire a brilliant idea during samone but have a terrible time finding out how to implement it during a delusional state. By staying aware of these states of our conscious mind, we can better keep centered and focused. We may both embrace the positive from these states and fight the negative. Most importantly, we can remind ourselves, that even when we die we still have a conscious mind.

1. Suneidesis

- Topics switch rapidly
- Can't make permanent decisions
- Easily distracted
- Difficult to absorb new ideas
- Mind is already made up

2. Samone

- New ideas process thoroughly
- Less mind chatter than suneidesis
- New things come easier than suneidesis
- Reflective and meditative
- Creative mindset
- Good for problem solving

3. Noetic

- More communicative than samone
- Not easily distracted
- Focused
- Easy to lose track of time
- Better for problem solving than samone
- Overrides primal instinct

4. Delusional

- Lose sense of discernment (places, direction, time, people)
- Usually caused by impairment (accidents, intoxication)
- Can be disorienting
- Hallucinations are possible
- Can forget identity and traits
- Often have grandiose ideas
- A small task can be a monumental undertaking

5. Delerium

- Severe disorientation
- Caused by hallucinogens
- Spacial orientation lost
- Unable to have clear and coherent thoughts
- Pills worsen condition

6. Comatose

- Physical body without connection to conscious mind
- Still has connection to supreme being
- Body cannot be woken
- Can exit with repair to cerebral cortex

7. Afterlife

- Spirit has left the body

Chapter 15 – The 31 Senses

Our body has many different senses that assist our conscious mind. Scholars have taught us that there are five primary senses. We may have heard that there is a sixth sense. It comprises all the things that we are not too sure about. In fact, there are not only five or six; we have *hundreds* of senses. The senses could fill a book alone; for now, we will cover the thirty-one primary senses. These are the senses that most affect your everyday life and help your spiritual consciousness.

Sight

Let us start with one of the most obvious senses, the one allowing us to read this right now. The sense of sight is an extremely useful and is shared by most living beings. In fact, it is critical to their very existence. Without sight, we could have some major issues.

Although there is plenty that an optometrist can do to improve vision, we can do much to improve it as well. If we find our eyes are getting weak, that we have trouble focusing or seeing out of our periphery, we can exercise our eyes. To improve our straight-ahead vision, choose a point about a foot away from our eyes and another point fifteen feet away. Focus back-and-forth between these two points. Bring each point fully into focus and then immediately look to the next point. As we do this, we'll find that at first, it will take a second or more to bring full detail into whatever we're focusing on. Likely, we'll notice that the distant point comes into focus faster than the near point. This simply means we're far-sighted, which is very common.

Repeat these back-and-forth repetitions fifteen times, twice a day. Ideally, we can practice this once in the morning, and once at night. Over time, we will find that the focus adjusts more quickly, and we will even notice more details. It may take months of practice before we find results that are more dramatic; this is normal. We're training not only your eyes, but the mind here; after all, it's the mind that instructs our eyes to focus. Like a practiced musician, we must repeat this exercise frequently. If we follow this regimen, we'll find that in a few short months we will have better vision and clearer focus.

For peripheral vision, extend the arms straight out in front with the palms of our hands facing down. Begin by wiggling our fingers and moving our hands arms slowly to the side. Keep the eyes locked straight as we continue to move the arms toward our sides. Do this until we can no longer see fingers wiggling. First, take note of where we first stopped seeing our fingers wiggle. If we repeat this exercise four or five times, twice daily, we will notice your peripheral vision improve. When we read a book, for instance, our eyes must refocus repeatedly as we move alone ac line. If we have poor peripheral vision, we may read slowly, or our eyes may become tired. The wider our peripheral vision, the fewer times we must refocus. With good enough peripheral vision, we can read an entire sentence without moving our eyes or refocusing. This greatly improves our ability to read, and it improves our ability to detect things in our peripheral vision that had previously gone unnoticed. For years, we may drive to work every day and not notice landmarks along the way. We are too focused straight ahead to enjoy anything in our peripheral vision. As your peripheral vision improves, we may notice things that are obvious but that we hadn't seen before. Have you ever caught a glimpse of something out of the corner of your eye? Often, it is our peripheral vision that allows us access to seeing energies in the 4th dimension, for example, auras and ghosts.

Hearing

A good sense of hearing can contribute tremendously to the quality of our life. We can test our hearing by paying attention while in nature. If we are not hearing birds, frogs, crickets, we may want to have a doctor peer into the ear and see if there is wax building up. It does become necessary to remove wax and not to rely on home remedies that could hurt the ears. Wax build-up is the most common reason for not getting a clear signal to the ear.

If we rely on high volume to hear, we are not exercising our ability to pick up sounds. To practice developing our hearing, turn down the volume of the radio or television. We may strain at first, but we will be making our ears work. In time, we will find yourself noticing new subtleties of sounds around us.

It is also important to protect the ears by wearing sound protection whenever we are around any loud noises such as lawnmowers, machinery, motorcycles, or even music. The most damaging sounds to the ears are motorized vehicles and gunshots; the ear has little tolerance for these things. If you're pounding a hammer on metal, for instance, it's wise to wear ear protection. Mechanics and other heavy laborers can completely lose their hearing in as short as twenty years if they are not careful to protect their ears.

The most pleasant noises to our ears are sounds like a babbling brook, ocean waves, and drops of rain. These natural sounds are harmonious and do nothing to damage the ear. These natural sounds are harmonious. If we want to practice hearing, sit or stand in nature during a calm, sunny day. We may have to go to a park or rural area. If we are unable to go to a natural area, then practice by turning down the volume of the television or radio. We may have to strain at first, but we will improve our hearing slowly. Focus intently and listen to the sounds; begin to pick out each sound. With practice, we will be hearing new sounds and notice things we were not even aware were out there. Hearing gives us greater awareness of our general surroundings and to keep us out of harm's way. These exercises will also help us to still the mind and assist us in hearing our spirit guides.

Touch

Although this is a major sense, we may not actually think about it that often. Look around the room for instance. We know what things look like, but if we were to close our eyes and concentrate on one object, we might not know what it feels like without first touching it. We all wear clothes, but may not like wearing items, and some people don't like wearing clothes at all. We are not sure why we don't, but it may be because they don't feel good on our skin. The best way to find out if we like the feeling of clothing is to close our eyes and feel the fabric before we buy it. If it has a pleasant feel, then go try the item on and see what the clothes feel like on the skin. If any part of it feels uncomfortable—too tight, constricting—then don't purchase it. If we are uncomfortable with anything we touch, we don't want to be around it.

Certain people don't like the feel of automotive grease on their fingers. These people would be wise not to become mechanics. Nevertheless, all too often, when I'm doing healings for people, they tell me that they don't like their jobs. When I ask what they don't like about their jobs, they say something such as, "I don't like working with greasy cars." They may say, "I don't like working with concrete because it pulls all the moisture out of my hands." If we don't like the feeling of something, we can have an uncomfortable experience. Concrete workers and automotive mechanics would benefit by wearing protective gloves to shield them from feelings they don't like. But strangely, there are people who don't take even small steps to remedy their situations. It is important to take the time to shield ourselves from unnecessary negative experiences.

Touch is a sense we can still improve upon. The first thing we can do is learn to touch others in ways that make them feel good. If someone likes his or her hair combed, it can be very bonding to use touch to feel closer to your partner. If someone likes their back rubbed, we should take the time to do some light massage on one another. It makes our life experience a lot more enjoyable and can improve our relationships. Still, we don't take the time to touch one another, even in simple gestures. We may encounter people who say they don't like being touched; but we will always find some degree of touching that's acceptable. Most people love to have back rubs, kisses or hugs. Even something as small as a hug, can bring about positive energies that allow a person to feel better about themselves. Being more sensitive to touch also helps us feel what our body is telling us about a situation. If something makes us feel a sense of constriction, then we may not want to be involved in it. The more in-tune you are with our bodies, the more able we will be to sense our intuition when it is occurring.

Smell

Smell is a safeguard mechanism that is given to us for our survival. A bad odor usually means 'stay away,' and a good odor usually means 'investigate further.' If we lose this ability, it might mean that there is something wrong metabolically in our body, or that we may have a pile-up of trapped emotions. No one is entirely sure why trapped emotions may interfere with the sense of smell, but I know that these emotions energetically cause interference and can lead to debilitating health. A deteriorating sense of smell may be nothing major, or it may be a sign of more serious problems.

The main reasons we would want to improve the sense of smell is either we have lost it or if it has been diminishing. The first thing we should do if we want to improve the sense of smell is investigate what allergies we have. A simple doctor's visit can address this. If we are aware of our allergies and know that they aren't causing diminished sense of smell, we may want to clear the sinus cavities. There are several ways this can be done. Doctors may recommend an antibiotic, but a sinus flush done with water may be a healthier way to resolve the issue. The sinus flush may hurt, but it is a quick and effective way to open the sinus passages.

Taste

Our taste depends a lot on the health of the taste buds on our tongue. There are people that have a diminished sense of taste, and this typically occurs as we age. Although people who lack a sense of taste can eat most any food, they may never get a warning that the body can't handle it or is allergic to a particular food. It could be the body doesn't need the food or they might develop an adverse reaction, such as people who don't like the taste of tomatoes. Taste can also alert us about whether something is ready to be eaten, or if it needs to mature. An immature fruit can cause difficulty in digestion and possibly cause food poisoning. If a food tastes particularly bad, it might be spoiled and should be avoided. Spoiled or outdated foods cause a primary reaction in the mouth but if we can't taste, of course, we might end up eating a toxic amount of it. The taste buds on our tongues are important as a survival mechanism. This was even more apparent before the advent of modern media, as we didn't have the Internet or news to warn us about poisoned or unhealthy foods. Animals, of course, are still using this as a survival mechanism.

People who have a heightened sense of taste often eat for pleasure. However, eating too often, can be unhealthy. The body needs time to digest what it has eaten. Our taste buds also add to our cravings, although most cravings are psychologically induced. A simple exercise for our taste buds is to suck on a hard piece of candy or chew gum. In some cases, this can even eliminate the craving to eat. Food will taste different on different parts of the tongue. Have you ever noticed that the first bite of something is the most delicious? The mechanism in place to curb our cravings gets satisfied with a very small amount of food. The body actually prefers a variety of food in small quantities, because this helps the body to get the balance of nutrients it needs. This is why food that is initially delicious may start to become less enjoyable after several bites.

Although the five previously listed senses of sight, sound, touch, and taste are the most commonly understood senses, they make up only a small part of our full spectrum of senses. Now, we will discuss some of the other lesser-known senses, the ones that aren't as well-known but vitally important.

Balance

Our sense of balance, also referred to as *equilibrioception*, relies heavily on sight. It is also highly affected by gravity and the strength of our muscles. We have seen how alcohol can affect someone's sense of balance. When balance is distorted, there is an eminent threat to the body. If the threat gets too large, such as the case with intoxication, the body may have to turn off the switch to the mind. We call this a blackout, and it occurs only when there is a threat of death. The superconscious mind does this for us. We can see what an important sense balance is.

If we've ever heard of someone being 'knocked senseless,' it's likely that they were hit so hard they temporarily lost their equilibrioception.

A simple way to improve our sense of balance is to stand on one leg and have someone push you just slightly. If we feel we are starting to teeter, we may have to use the other leg to regain balance. Repeat the process by having someone push you again with the same amount of force, and this time you might stand in place more steadily. This is because the brain is catching up to the signal of being pushed. It will regain equilibrioception rather quickly, whereas the first experience caught us a little off-guard. The body constantly strives to maintain perfect equilibrioception. If we find you cannot stand on one foot, we may also want to try yoga to improve balance. When I was a young man, I went to a yoga class held at a senior citizens' center. I was amazed at how poor my balance was compared to some of the much older people. Your equilibrioception does not degenerate with age unless you allow it to. The more we practice yoga postures, the better we become and the less likely we are to fall unexpectedly. I have met younger people who seem to be always falling; they lack strong equilibrioception.

Focus

Focus is a sense, but many people may never have thought of it as such. Distractions themselves are not a sense, but our sense of focus determines how well we cope with them. As one would expect, focus is closely tied to our emotional state. People who are nervous have a tough time coping with distractions, and often create their own distractions, so in a sense they are their own worst enemy.

When a beautiful woman walks past a man, he can get distracted quite easily, which can result in getting smacked by his wife! When we know we are to be working or studying, we might distract ourselves by making extra trips to the fridge or being engaged in silly television shows. Sometimes people might have a hard time focusing at a movie theater and get angry because the people nearby them are whispering. We all deal with various distractions in different ways.

When I was traveling through California once, I couldn't help but notice all the garbage along the highway. I was disturbed that the road looked like a giant garbage pit. I began to feel judgmental, and it was difficult to enjoy the trip. I had to redirect my thinking to something more positive. I had let those distractions ruin my experience until I came up with a better method of dealing with them. Sneezing, coughing, a loud clap, a passing car, people talking near you and the wind are just some of the many things that can distract and disrupt the thinking process. When we learn to eliminate the distractions by using the power of our mind, we can master distractions and use them to our own advantage. If we are trying to read in a busy cafeteria and we could clump together the sounds around us, treating them as background white noise, rather than as multiple individual distractions then the distractions would not be so disturbing. Some people find white noise helpful in focusing, using a fan or a noise generator to help them to sleep or concentrate. These distractions might still be a problem for others, but our ability to cope with them will ensure that we can enhance our ability to focus and accomplish more.

People who are easily distracted may never complete projects and feel that they have become failures. Successful people are not easily distracted and even love a challenge. They work effectively in environments where others might find it impossible to be creative. I have witnessed uncompleted projects my whole life. The people just became distracted, and they could no longer organize their multiple demands. Perhaps if they had developed methods of managing distractions, instead of feeling like failures, they could enjoy the pride of a job well-done! The ability to focus also helps one to clear the mind, making it easier to hear from spirit guides.

Thermoception

Thermoception, the sense of temperature, is important because the body only survives within a certain external temperature range. Some researchers have erroneously believed that we are born with this sense, but today we understand that it is at least partially learned. When a child touches a hot burner the sense of temperature will kick in, but the child may take a few seconds to pull back. It is a long way from the sensors in the hand to the brain, and then the brain must process this information and send a response back to the hand.

If humans lost the sense of temperature, our species would quickly perish. For example, if we were to go swimming in a lake that was near freezing and we had no sense of the temperature, how long would we survive? Not long, as hypothermia would set in quickly. The Universal Creator would become frustrated, having made a being that could never live to reproduce. This would not be a winning combination, even if everything else about the being were perfect, it would not survive without a sense of thermoception. We take this sense for granted, but how do we control it? It's quite straightforward. The mind can set its desired limit at a certain temperature. We also can expand those limits.

To accept temperatures outside of the normal range, meditate and concentrate intently in a quiet place. Tell yourself repeatedly that you are expanding your range. Ideally, you should be specific; if you are in a colder climate, think to yourself, "I am expanding my thermoception to bear 20 degrees." Fortunately, this can change in a matter of minutes. If you repeat to yourself a mantra, staying focused on getting yourself prepared, you will be able to shortly enter whatever temperature you've prepared yourself for. It may not be perfect; you may still sweat in hot weather and shiver in the cold. However, you'll find that your mind can bear the temperature for a longer time than you would have previously. If you've moved to a new climate, try to repeat this mantra every time you prepare to go outside; in a matter of a month—sometimes even a week—you will be outside, enjoying the weather like the locals.

I don't know how many times I have heard people say that they cannot take the cold. Ultimately, this isn't true; according to the spirit world, this just means that the person is unwilling to expand the limits of his or her comfort zone. People who grow up in cold climates have never been programmed to think that the cold was uncomfortable. They may not feel the need to wear protective clothing at temperatures that a person who is used to extreme heat could hardly bear.

Consider the example of firewalking. The temperature is the same for every person, but some of them will be unharmed, while others could be burned. The mind plays an important part in what we allow into our body. If we repel enough of the heat by using the power of the mind, it doesn't seem to hurt us. I will admit that I haven't gotten over my own phobia of fire, so I don't blame anyone that will not attempt to fire walk.

I will give another quick example of thermoception. If we rub our hands until they got hot, and then hold the palms close, moving them away and together again, we will feel the thermoception between them.

Homeostasis

Homeostasis is a term for maintaining the body's internal temperature. This too is a sense. The body could control its temperature at 98.6 Fahrenheit, or 37 degrees Celsius. When a virus or a bacterium enters the body, the temperature will rise to a higher level to kill the virus. Too high a temperature can kill cells.

We can control the temperature inside us with the power of thought. Gifted individuals across the world have demonstrated their abilities to lower or raise their own body temperatures. As we might guess from this, homeostasis is a function of our spirit, rather than our body.

This sense works together with thermoception. When we enter a hot climate, our external impulses let us know that there is a high heat present. The mind will automatically lower our bodies temperature to adjust for the presence of the heat. If we ask your superconscious mind to allow in the heat, such as people do in a sauna, the heat will build until it becomes too uncomfortable to withstand. The body will let us know when it is time to refrain from the activity in the form of a headache or chills. We have enormous control over homeostasis, but we should respect its limitations.

How do we maintain a constant temperature? By giving the body enough water each day, we can control the internal temperature. The fact is, most animals dehydrate quickly and do then not operate at optimum efficiency. Dehydration leads to a higher temperature and that can lead to rapid aging. We can also change your body's temperature by movement, or lack thereof. If we're cold, even something as simple as huddling; if we're hot, sitting still in the shade can make all the difference.

Know that there are limits to what our body can do to regulate our temperature. If it's blazingly hot outside, only so much water and psychological resilience can protect us. If we get so hot that we feel chilled, or so cold that we feel hot, we are hitting your physical limits and must take steps to protect ourselves immediately.

Pressure

Our sense of *pressure* is a very important sense. Our internal pressure is determined by our genetic makeup. The medical community measures pressure in the circulatory system and it has long been thought to be an indicator of health. Although this is partially correct, different species vary in their abilities to control their blood pressure. Many species—including humans—control blood pressure through the process of sleep. Sleep is one of the most essential factors in maintaining a stable blood pressure. Also, the higher the degree of impurities in the blood and the vessels that carry the blood to vital organs, the higher the blood pressure will climb. It compensates for any restrictions or impurities.

Our sense of external pressure is part of our sense of pressure. For example, how tightly we grip a young infant to keep them from falling out of our arms is a pressure sense. Our nervous system regulates our touch sensors, and we learn through trial and error what pressure to apply to hold something. Without the sense of pressure, we would not have been able to excel in evolutionary development. We would not be able to use tools or writing instruments. We would even find it challenging to type on a keyboard without destroying the keys. Just imagine how difficult it would be trying to play a harp or a violin without a sense of pressure.

When someone gets angry it affects this sense, and that can affect other senses. When we get angry your blood pressure rises and our nervous system gets taxed. The next time we get angry; please remember that we are messing with the sense of pressure.

If we suffer from high blood pressure, anger, or a neck injury, acupressure is an effective way for the body to reprogram its pressure. In any of these cases, the sense of pressure gets discordant, and the body has to go through a process of recalibrating. This is part of the reason that we need sleep. When we sleep, our sense of pressure recalibrates. Each cell in the body depends upon the proper amount of pressure.

To control the sense of pressure we need a sleep program that is consistent and makes us feel refreshed and ready to tackle the world. Too much sleep can throw us off the same way that too little sleep can. If we keep a daily sleep log, we will soon find the pattern that works the best for us.

Air Pressure

Air pressure is a sense that is measured in the human body and can result in pain or discomfort in the sinuses, the ears, or the nerves in the brain. Too much air pressure, as experienced by divers deep within the ocean, can result in death to the human vessel. Too little pressure, as seen at high altitudes, can result in damage to the central nervous system. Loud noises increase air pressure, which can result in damage to the ear, in response, the ear increases its internal pressure to keep the eardrum from breaking. This is a complex problem. If the ear allows too much sound into the eardrum, then deafness can occur. When a person becomes deaf, many of their senses can become affected. There are air pockets around every vital organ that detect air pressure. If the pressure becomes too great, the individual can even suffer from a temporary disruption in the flow of blood from the heart to the brain. Places with continuously loud noises can affect all the organs due to the impact that the noise has on air pressure. These places should be avoided at all costs. Think about how important proper air pressure is in your car tires. Our bodies air pressure is critical, not just in the lungs but also in each individual cell. Our cell vitality is directly related to the proper pressure.

What can we do to adjust our air pressure? There are many things, ranging from making sure that we don't have too much wax build up in our ears to expelling negative thoughts that get trapped in our energy matrix. Our emotional state greatly affects the air pressure in our body but just how that occurs is a bit beyond our current levels of comprehension.

Kinesiology

This is also known as the science of human movement. We work with and hone this sense in orthopedics, strength conditioning, sports psychology, and rehabilitation, such as physical and occupational therapy. The Greeks first understood that kinesiology was a sense, and they had a science that evolved around it. They knew that it was therapeutic and felt it had magical properties. The word even comes from the Greek words' *kinesis*, which means 'movement.' If we feel we must improve our kinesiology, try taking up yoga or walking.

[You must be careful about people trying to sell us things to 'improve' this sense. For Example, some state that wearing magnetic bands will help the sense of movement or balance. Although these people claim to help our kinesiological sense, they're only taking advantage of our equilibrioception. They may attempt to push us once without their bracelet, and then again with it. The second time, obviously, we'll be prepared for the push; as discussed above, our equilibrioception will have kicked in. This has nothing to do with magnetism or the health of our kinesiological sense; these are just people trying to sell their wares.]

Telepathy

Telepathy, or communicating by thought, is another sense that each human has, but may not know how to use. Telepathy comes from the ancient Greek word *pathe* meaning a feeling, perception, passion, or experience. Another term we use for this is "thought transference." We telepathically communicate with humans, spirits, and even animals. I don't think we could convince pet owners otherwise. According to the spirit world, telepathy is one of the most common forms of communication in the Universe. Telepathy is not, as some fantasies portray, the direct ability to hear what another person is thinking. Rather it is the implicit understanding of another person's feelings or thoughts, the non-verbal communication that occurs between two people. What many would consider 'empathy' is one aspect of telepathy.

Some researchers have to great lengths to prove that telepathy is just delusional thinking and a sign of schizoaffective disorder. This is why there are so few studies done in the field of telepathy. People who believe they have telepathic abilities have been labeled as "crazy" and treated with antipsychotic medications, when they should have been embraced and enlisted to help the telepathic abilities of others.

If we want to test our telepathic abilities, find a friend—or ideally, a group of friends—and lay down six playing cards face-up in front of them. Allow one person to choose one of the six cards and instruct them to focus only on that card. The others involved should then attempt to guess which card the person is envisioning. Chance would predict that the guesses would be correct only one in six times, but interestingly, the odds tend to err closer to 50 percent or even 75 percent for particularly telepathic individuals. We can use this test to both find out how naturally telepathic we are and to further develop our skills.

Body Language

Body language is a sense that can be felt emotionally by others. A speaker that has great body language will have an enormous impact on his or her audience compared to one with poor body language. The speaker may be said to have charisma. Good charisma is partially due to appropriate body language. Body language should be targeted for the audience. Crossed arms indicate a closed-minded listener, and no one wants to speak to a closed-minded individual. Slouching indicates a lack of interest or disdain about the subject matter that is being discussed. When a speaker slouches they are usually considered uninteresting by the audience. A speaker who is trembling would appear to be in fear and would not inspire audiences as much as one that is perceived as confident. A speaker with a turned down mouth is sad and may not be effective at driving home a point.S

When people have a difficult time looking us in the eye it can be hard to trust what is being said. This can be misinterpreted, because in some cultures people consider it impolite to stare. The distance that we stand from someone when talking is a big part of body language. If people are standing too close or talking too loudly, it can be interpreted as an invasion of the others private space. These people might be viewed by another as being too aggressive, overbearing, or hostile.

Body language can be practiced. Those who practice it the most are usually the most successful people. It is a sense that can be controlled.

Synesthesia

Synesthesia is not only a sense unto itself, but also what happens when we stimulate one sense and discover that other senses have begun to improve with it. We likely have heard of this phenomenon as a neurological condition, where people can 'taste' sounds or see colors on numbers or letters. Nevertheless, these are individuals who are extremely sensitive; everyone has this sense to some degree. This is something that occurs at the cellular level that improves and heightens another sense.

To give another example, if one hears a song and it incites the ability to see into another dimension, or it reminds them of a visualization or smell, it is just a normal process of this sense being stimulated. Although we all can do this, only a minority of people perceive this sense daily. Most of us either are unaware that we have this ability, or we prefer not to stimulate it. If we are thinking of happy thoughts while smelling food, that is a direct function of synesthesia at work. Some realtors will take advantage of this sense in the process of showing a home for sale. They will bake bread in the home just before an open house. It gives the buyer a warm home feeling that they may relate to positively. Synesthesia should not be considered a mysterious sense. It is one that we all have, but may not yet be aware of.

Breathing

Breathing is a sense, not just a response. We have a direct sense how much to breathe and whether to breathe; if we are running, we will breathe faster; if we fall into water, we know—even as babies—not to breathe. Although it seems to be automatic, we can control our breathing greatly. This is one of the strongest senses. We breathe more shallowly when we are exposed to polluted air than we do when we are in fresh air. This is a learned sense and can be improved upon. The art of breathing has been taught for thousands of years by many cultures.

Breathing is a process that moves air in and out of the body. All aerobic organisms do this and it results in a process of metabolism called respiration. If we increase our breathing we burn more calories, and thus we can control how much energy we use in a day depending upon on how we breathe. Heavy people often breath shallow and get by with the fewest possible breaths required to sustain themselves. This is quite dangerous because breathing delivers oxygen to the body wherever it is needed and removes carbon dioxide. Oxygen is important to the bloodstream so that our blood purifies itself. Oxygen also energizes the body and is used in countless biochemical reactions throughout the body. The deeper we breathe, the more oxygen we send to the entire body.

Most of us in society have become shallow breathers. It's not that we don't know how to breathe; it's that we don't breathe enough to oxygenate our body properly. We can improve breathing by practiced breathing, meditation, or yoga. A very big part of yoga and many martial arts center around controlled, deep breathing. Expert singers learn to control their breathing. We can direct your breath to any part of our body we desire; although this may seem surprising, it is proven to be true. For instance, if we find ourselves not thinking clearly, we can attempt to direct more oxygen to the brain. Take deep breaths and imagine that our oxygen-rich blood is flowing upward to the head. If you imagine this for about a minute, we may begin to find ourselves clearer-headed, able to think more quickly. We can also direct our breath into a stiff area of the body to relax the muscles.

Eating and Drinking

Eating and drinking are critical senses. The digestive system is complex and the overabundance of food in our modern society is dangerous to our health. Our body can tell us how much to eat and drink, but if we eat and drink too fast the message does not get to the brain in time to let us know that we are full. Overeaters are usually just eating too fast, or they are not taking the time to chew their food long enough. Eating and drinking has become a social activity and not based on the body's needs.

How much we feel we must eat, and drink is largely a result of our body sending messages to our brain. These messages generate our thoughts. The two senses can unfortunately get easily confused with one another. For example, sometimes when we think we are hungry, we might actually be thirsty instead. That's why the senses of eating and drinking are combined.

In order to pay attention to our senses of hunger and thirst, we need to focus on how we're feeling. If we're feeling tired for no reason, we either have not enough sustenance, or we have eaten so much that the body is having a difficult time recuperating. If we don't pay enough attention to our body's need for water, then we become dehydrated and listless.

Our body will let us know that there is something wrong with our sense of eating and drinking by giving us cravings, though at times, some of times the things we crave may keep us from achieving optimum health. A craving is really a signal from our body that something is wrong, and we will often misinterpret what we should be eating. Still this sense is quite important, and we should try to tune into our bodies signals better.

Speech

The sense of speech refers to more than using language to communicate with others. It explains that we make noises at all, and that we instinctively use certain noises in certain situations. When we stub our toe, often we make some sound. That verbal output is a result of the action, (stubbing our toe) that stimulated our sense of speech. When we hear a sound, we may try to mimic that sound. This is especially true as a child. How often have you heard a child make the noise of a tractor when they're playing with a toy tractor?

All words spoken should be carefully weighed by both the speaker and the receiver since people will react differently to the same words based upon the situation. Much of what we say is also processed in different ways depending on our cultural upbringing, and many words have the power to make or break the individual hearing them.

Knowing when to use verbal inputs and how to use them is a sense. How we control our verbal comments can be a learned portion of this equation. Young people can be taught to not let words have power over them. Many of our youth are coerced into doing something because of what someone has said. In their desire to be popular with others, they will sometimes do things suggested by others without a rational explanation. If the words do not resonate with us, then do not allow them to control or influence our lives. This is a sense that we do have enormous control of, and we should use it wisely.

Sense of Time

The *sense of time* is one that frequently gets distorted. We can easily lose track of time depending on how preoccupied we become with a hobby or item of interest. This is one reason that humans became dependent on using clocks or nowadays checking their cell phones to get the exact time. Although we can become tied to exact time as a measure of our responsibility, we can get too caught up in it.

I'm familiar with cases in which people knew they are about to die. How could this be? These people had a sense that their time was running out. Not because of how ill they were feeling but because they felt, they no longer had anything to do. They had just gotten to the point that they understood that their lives were now completed. The sense of time ties into this feeling and our sense of life spans are closely related to our electrical functions.

Jet lag is quite common among travelers. This can really affect one's sense of time. The brain is wired with a sense of time that we call our internal clock. Our internal clock can be set to wake us at a specific time without the use of an alarm clock, but it is up to us to program in the "wake up" time. Our internal clock needs to be reset after we have gone through a cold or brief illness. Our ancestors were aware of the movements of the sun and the stars, and through this method, they were able to pinpoint the exact time of day and the time of the month. Although, since the introduction of the calendar, this ability has been nearly forgotten. However it remains a latent sense that we can restore if we choose to.

Gravity

We have a sense of gravity; that is, we know and can feel which way the world is pulling on us. The revolution of the moon around the Earth every twenty-seven and one-third days creates gravitational changes in our oceans which in turn affects our weather patterns. The human menstrual cycle is also linked to this lunar cycle, and all animals and sea creatures are affected by the varying gravitational pull from our moon. Incidentally our Earth along with all the other planets, are being drug behind the Sun at an alarming speed

Each person has a built-in genetic sequence that helps them adjust to gravity. This sense can be greatly affected when traveling from one altitude to another. Air travel has the most impact because you are changing the gravitational pull changes so abruptly. At altitudes of 30,000 feet the gravitational field is weaker than at sea level and astronauts traveling in space experience nearly a complete absence of gravity! The body can have trouble adjusting to the sudden gravitational changes and once an airplane has landed passengers must quickly adjust to the stronger gravity. Many people may even feel ill until they fully adjust to the change, and astronauts returning from space may take weeks to readjust.

Note: *It is not recommended to travel from one continent to another for a period of less than twenty to thirty days, but of course we don't have a way to counteract this. Most people travel for a period of seven to nine days as this is as much vacation time as they are allowed but in this short period their body may not have fully recovered from the effects of gravity.*

Chapter 15 – The 31 Senses

Electroception

The sense of *electroception* is a sense that we take entirely for granted. It is the ability to detect any electrical activity. People can feel a tingling sensation in their hand or body when this sense is activated. The signals in the brain are about one hundred microvolts. They have frequencies of about one to twenty hertz or cycles per second. The signals in the heart are about ten times greater than that of the brain. Even though these signals are hard to detect, they can still be measured. Healers can transfer up to five millivolts per second, which is five times greater than the electrical energy of the heart. Most healers will transmit ten to fifty microvolts per second, and at that frequency many people will not be able to notice the effect of the transfer. A five millivolt per second session will result in a whirl of activity that will be felt throughout the body. The next time we have a chance to feel the electrical energy from a person or an animal try to focus the mind on the impulse. If we can feel it we have activated our electrical sense.

Scire Spatium

Scire spatium is a sense of knowing our distance from objects. We are not born with this sense fully developed, and it varies between species. Eagles have a heightened sense of scire spatium. For instance, they can tell just how far below its prey is. We don't see them diving down to the ground and going splat; oops, there's the ground! They have mastered this sense because it is necessary for their survival.

Humans pale in comparison to eagles about our scire spatium abilities, though many athletes have cultivated this sense. We can all practice the following exercises to have scire spatium. First, walk up to a wall and then stop when we are close enough to reach out with the hand and touch the wall. If at first we are off, try it again until we are successful. To work on this long-range sense let's say we see a parked car in the distance. We might try to estimate how many paces it will take us to reach it. The first time we may be off by a great deal but with practice, we may be able to judge within a pace or two.

Scire Post

Knowing that there is something behind us is another so called sixth sense that we call *scire post*. Objects emit energy that gives away their position. We can detect and interpret this energy. The more we practice this sense, the better we can become at identifying the objects that are behind us.

The blind often demonstrate this ability. Some have referred to this as having eyes in the back of our head.

Cultivating Cultural Practices

People feel the need to fit into a culture. Cultivating cultural practices is a sense that helps us to do that. We can judge if our actions are acceptable to society. Washing hands before a meal, saying grace, or taking off shoes at the door are examples of cultural practices. Such shared practices make it easier for individuals to function within a society.

A society labels one behavior as acceptable and the next as unacceptable. Unacceptable behavior is usually dealt with by the penal system. The penal system took many years to develop, and it is constantly changing. In the days of the cowboy, it was considered bad behavior to ride a horse into a bank or a saloon. People wouldn't even imagine something like that of in today's time, but back then it was a problem and required specific laws to prevent or punish that behavior. Children demonstrate the ability to cultivate cultural practices when testing new actions by gauging their parents' responses. Culture sometimes allows unacceptable behaviors if the behaviors do no harm to others. Extremely unacceptable behaviors may not be forgiven in politics but would be tolerated from entertainers. Entertainers can even behave inappropriately to gain fame.

This sense is important because it helps us to discern between right and wrong. People at a young age instinctively know right from wrong even though they were not taught these things. This understanding is built into the conscious mind. The ability to know right from wrong is further refined by exercising the cultivation of cultural practices.

Energy Pheromones

Here is a weird sense: the ability to detect and interpret secretions and body excrements from others. This isn't simply a sense of smell: this is sensing the *energetic* release from a body's secretions. When we are sick or tired, for example, our bodies will emit secretions that send messages to others around us. Secretions are sent for a variety of reasons that include mating, warning against disease, and keeping us away from pain. Our ability to sense when there is danger is a function of our sense of secretion. Interpreting these sensations depends upon our whole-body receptors. There are millions of these receptors throughout the body. Some secretions act as warning signals to us by activating our olfactory senses. Excretions like urine and sweat can indicate the degree of health in the body. For example, when animals or humans become ill, their sweat glands emit odors that might not be initially detectable by the nose but will be acknowledged by other receptors. Unpleasant odors are an indication of infection and presence of parasites, the stronger the odor, the stronger the message. Another function of the ability to detect secretions is much more positive. It's not a warning of danger but can be used as reproductive stimulus. When these senses are stimulated, it can result in an increased heartbeat, faster breathing, or increased level of cortisol production. It can elevate the mood, or even sexually excite another person.

Secret-keeping

The *ability to keep a secret* is a sense. Our nature is to share exciting information. The ability to keep from divulging secrets is a learned skill. I know people who have a really hard time with this. Facebook is a way of getting rid of your secrets. I recommend using it if we want the world to know our secrets. How often has someone told us a huge secret and we couldn't wait to share it with at least one other person. Well, that person likely has another person that they want to tell it to, then before long the whole secret has become a world-wide public event. For movie stars this is certainly the case. So, if we have the desire to hold secrets for someone we might well have full-time work.

We have emotions such as guilt, that are highly connected to the sense of danger and fear. For example, let's say that we have a contractual obligation at our job to keep something a secret. If one violates this promise, one may experience a sense of guilt. One could even be fired from his or her job and even be prevented from working a similar job for a different company. This secret keeping may not be as easy as it sounds.

To reinforce citizens ability to keep secrets, governments may use a threat of incarceration. Some government agencies have even devised tests that measure an individual's ability to maintain secrets. Some people are gifted with this sense at birth, and others have no such ability or desire.

Empathy

Empathic abilities are defined as the ability to get a sense or understanding of what another being is feeling. Animals can be empathic, and if we think about it, a dog seems to sense when we are unhappy. The dog will make a concerted effort to communicate its love for us. Its empathy is powerful and uplifting.

The act of feeling the emotions of another individual is a common example of empathic psychic ability and can lead to positive understandings between people. I know people who can get so empathically involved with the overwhelming emotions of another, they become emotionally exhausted or drained. Empathics must learn to manage their own responses to the many emotions that they can sense from others or risk burnout. Here is a technique that I teach to clients when I am working with them on their emotions. This approach can also be used by empathics. Tell our superconscious mind that we want to release a negative emotion that seems to be stuck in us. Know that it is not defining who we are. It does not belong to us. It does not serve us. Release this emotion and let it go. So be it. We will be able to feel the trapped energy leave the body and there will be lightness around it now.

Intuition

Intuition is a sense, defined as a feeling or hunch that one has that does not come from an outside source. Like all senses, intuitive powers may vary. Some highly intuitive people even feel bothered by the effects of their strong sense. Intuition manifests itself in several ways; if we have a strong intuitive sense, we may find ourselves able to know what to heal on others. Our intuition may lead us to see potential pathways into a person's future. In general, the intuitive sense can take advantage of light, color and sound.

We can sharpen your sense of intuition. The primary way to do that is through our dreams. Each time we go to sleep, the mind passes from the waking state to the sleeping dream. When the mind passes into the dream state, we have an opportunity to sort things out from the subconscious mind. If we remember these dreams and are half-awake, it is called lucid dreaming. In a lucid dream, we can take control of the dream and even influence it. In this way, the dreamer can practice changing the dream, instead of the dreamer only reacting to the dream. Changing the dream is one of the first steps of manifestation and it is one of the most integral parts of intuition. When we can change our dream in the dream state to better reflect our wants and desires, we are affecting our subconscious decisions. These subconscious decisions enhance our abilities to develop our psychic and intuitive senses.

Light can improve our intuitive sense as well. Sunlight is the most powerful form of light and it is recommended that we spend as much time as possible in the sun. It is important to expose our entire body to the sun

Chapter 15 – The 31 Senses

for at least twenty minutes per day. Those who have more sunlight exposure tend to be more intuitive.

Intuitive senses are also improved by the addition of color into our daily regime. By wearing beautiful, bright colors, we begin emitting higher-than-normal energies. Wearing colors—or even being in a brightly colored room—opens a channel of energy that conducts with vibrancy, and it becomes easier for us to derive energy from the sun.

Sound has a large impact on intuitive senses. Musicians often display exaggerated psychic abilities because they can process sound easily and their enjoyment of music becomes greater. The more inspiring music that a person listens to the greater their psychic abilities will become. I will have a chapter later to get into more detail about intuition.

Remote Sensing

Remote sensing is sometimes labeled as an extra-sensory perception (ESP). We have detectors throughout the body that can sense many types of things at a distance. For example, remote sensing includes abilities like remote hearing, remote tasting, and even remote viewing. People have an ability to hear things thousands of miles away by projecting their energies to distant locations. There have been government programs that experimented with these remote senses. Remote viewing was used in war time to find out information such as the size and location of enemy forces. Although it was largely experimental, opened a new field of science that has intrigued thousands of individuals who study the paranormal.

The human body is also equipped with motion and wave detectors. These receptors are in the skin and can detect motion even when the body is asleep. It is a form of ESP which is sometimes referred to in the general sense, as the sixth sense. Perhaps this field requires more exploration. What the eye cannot see, can still be felt, and with this talent the human species could become more connected to the spiritual world.

Subliminal Senses

Humans have *subliminal senses*. Subliminal means *below the threshold*. In this case, subliminal senses are 'below the threshold' of other senses. In some ways, you can see subliminal senses as more subtle versions of other, more prominent senses. Researchers have found that subliminal messages may have at most, brief impacts on our behavior. About this, they are dead wrong. We are a society of people who want all the things everything that is advertised whether we will make use of them or not. We have been programmed subliminally to want things we don't even need. We are not aware that we are being brainwashed by advertisers because the subliminal inputs are below the threshold for conscious perception. Still there is an urge to purchase something that we really don't need but the desire was created by unscrupulous advertisers.

Subliminal stimuli do activate specific regions of the brain despite participants being unaware. Such things as visual stimuli can be processed by the brain at incredible speeds, in the range of one million characters per second. Subliminal audio stimuli can also be understood by the brain. They are played below audible volumes and can be masked by other stimuli. We can use this to your advantage if we want to learn something quickly; play an audio book or lesson on low volume while we sleep. Your subliminal senses will receive the input and process while we sleep.

Some people can sense heat across distances and locate and identify the pitch of a sound. Musicians use this sense to recreate the music that they hear another play. Some researchers have called this an extra sensory perception and put it into a broad category. Shamans use the subliminal senses to a greater degree than the masses do. They can, for example, sense where animals have passed through an area and how many of them there were. They can move into the astral body and detect what illnesses a person has, and in many cases change their picture of reality. This is done by tapping into the subliminal sense. *Sublime* is defined as the quality of greatness or vast magnitude whether it be intellectual, metaphysical, aesthetic or artistic.

Particle Detection

Humans are equipped with a sense that can detect particles and their charges at the subatomic level. Some researchers refer to this as micro psi. Papers were published about these micro particles even before the invention of the electron microscope. There have been many cultures, such as India, that understood that there was a microscopic world and spoke of it in their ancient legends. Modern books on Indian Yoga mention psychic powers or "*siddhis*" which a yogi may attain because of meditation. It has been written that a Yogi can acquire knowledge of small, hidden or distant stimuli. What they are doing is tapping into the particle detection sense. It is a more rarely used ESP sense than some of the others.

Meditation is a way of mastering particle detection. When we meditate, we can send or receive particles and these particles can be directed. For example, we can send love to another person, we can send healing energies, and we can even send information. Particle detection can be useful in eliminating disease in the body and to make things behave the way we would like them to behave. Under a microscope it is easier to see how our thoughts impact things at the cellular level.

Neural Signals

Neural signals are senses that have been rarely examined. They are largely a part of the macroscopic realm, but we have been given a bit of this ability to produce and modify neural signals. The ability to convert mechanical, chemical and electromagnetic energy into neural signals that have meaningful thought is one of the human senses. Neural signals are the electrical potential carrying the information to be transmitted between neurons or dendrites. Researchers are just beginning to understand how the brain processes the information that it receives, but yet have no concept of how these signals get converted into thought. All stimuli have components that have to be interpreted by the brain before they can be acted upon. This sense can be very useful in remote healing but if the power is abused it can be destructive as well. We should work with caution when practicing this ability.

Chapter 16 – The Superconscious Mind

The largest part of our mind is the superconscious mind, and it is least understood. It comprises 88 percent of the three minds. This is the part of our mind that's connected to our spirit. As we've seen, the conscious mind is like the eyes of the soul, interfacing us with the physical realm. The superconscious mind interfaces us with the spirit. Most people are not aware of the functions their superconscious mind has to offer them. Even if we were told one day that we had a superconscious mind, the question that comes to mind is - what is it and how do we use it?

The superconscious mind is what makes the most important decisions in our lives. For example, the superconscious mind is the one that helps us find our personal interests, our career choices, and even the people we choose to associate. Our conscious choices, affected as they are by the various states of mind we might be in, are not always healthy ones. Our superconscious mind, on the other hand, has our best interests at heart. The spirit world contains, among other things, all the experiences of an individual and the information that it has learned. This information is stored in an energetic library that our superconscious mind can access.

The superconscious mind is our direct link to our soul and the spirit world. Our superconscious mind is a part of everyone, not of an outside force, but a component of our spirits. There is a misconception that the superconscious mind is a higher form or wiser part of our own consciousness.

The superconscious mind comprises 88 percent of properties related to the multidimensional nature of your soul, such as: astral travel, manifestations, psychic abilities, mental time travel, connecting with the Akashic records, and more. The other twelve percent of the superconscious mind is comprised of components that help maintain a balance between your physical and spiritual natures, and they are named the ego, Illogism, and superego. Understanding the superconscious mind's components and how they function will offer us the power to steer our lives in ways we may have only dreamed of. The superconscious mind is so-called because it is much greater than the conscious mind. Our conscious mind plays a small role in comparison.

Ultimately, the superconscious mind is our direct connection to God. This manifests itself in numerous ways. In many cultures, we see prayers and affirmations as a big part of getting what we want, in making life better for everyone. In recent years, there has been a surge of interest in positive thinking, affirmations, and manifesting. All these things, from prayer and affirmations to simply thinking a lot about what we want in life, function because of the power of the superconscious mind.

One of its most useful functions is the ability to manifest our desires. We can call on our superconscious mind for almost anything that we would like or to obtain or change in our lives, but we first must realize that we have this ability. It relays our prayers and desires to the spirit world for processing into manifestations. If one desires to become healthier, more attractive, or more intelligent, he or she can ask the superconscious mind to assist but know that it is a gradual process. The superconscious will process the communication or request in three ways. It will alert the soul of its desire, send messages to the subconscious mind to help create new beliefs for making new realities, and it will send messages to the conscious mind to remind it to stay focused on the request. The Universe will then start attracting into our lives the required help to manifest our desires. If the conscious mind desires something that the superconscious mind knows is not in the best interest of the soul, the request is not fulfilled.

The superconscious mind is also busy operating our physical autopilot programs. These autopilot programs, such as the autonomic nervous system was put into place to keep the body functioning properly. When we ask our superconscious mind for help with something, we should not forget to mention that it should do this as a secondary request to its main priorities. For example, let's say for instance that we would like some help filling in the face wrinkles so that people will perceive us as younger. But what if the heart is ailing that day? We should ask it to continue to run the crucial programs, so things such as the heart will get the healing it requires. Compared to the heart, wrinkles are not the critical concerns. The superconscious mind waits for us to finish our requests so that it can begin operating. We might say something like, 'amen,' or, 'so be it,' to let the superconscious mind know that it may begin the process.

Of all prayers that we request via the superconscious mind, our requests that are made for health are the most often granted. As the body is the vessel, the tool of the conscious mind, it is only logical that the superconscious mind is more willing to consider the body's health before, say, extraordinary wealth.

However, it's important to know that, in some cases, the spirit might have requested that we experience a specific disease to complete a soul contract lesson. In these cases, our ailments may not be so easily reversed. However, we do have the ability to rewrite these contracts. This can be

Chapter 16 – The Superconscious Mind

achieved through prayer. Prayer is one of the most powerful tools we can implement. If we combine the use of other people praying for us, the results can be more impactful. So, when we put it out to the Universe exactly what our desires are, and we are asking the spirit world to assist us, the superconscious mind takes our requests more seriously.

We might be new to the concept of rewriting our soul contracts. I have seen people rewrite contracts and watched them change remarkably. Instead of being simply cured of a specific disease, we may be encouraged to act differently, and those behavioral changes will heal a variety of disorders. To recover from a specific disease, we might be encouraged to eat differently, travel to another region of the country, change our work environments, and even let go of some toxic relationships that may not be serving us. We may be given ways to heal emotional traumas or change negative distorted beliefs. If we choose not to cooperate with these promptings or heed the messages that we get from our spirit guides, changes may not occur. It is important that we prove to the superconscious mind, and therefore to the spirit world at large, that we want what we are requesting. We must demonstrate that we are willing to make the required changes.

The superconscious mind may, in some contexts, be construed as the 'secret,' as the 'Holy Ghost,' as 'God' itself. In fact, the superconscious mind is a part of *you*, not of an outside force. It is our connection to the spirit which in turn accesses manifesting power from the soul. Since our superconscious mind is the direct connection to the soul, and the soul is the direct connection to the Universal Creator, then it would be okay to pray to God, because our superconscious mind knows what we are asking for. The superconscious transmits the prayer to the Universal Creator. In the next section, we are going to talk more about techniques and teachings that will make our connection to the superconscious mind easier. It begins by praying to the superconscious.

Praying to Your Superconscious Mind

The superconscious mind can be compared to a computer processor. Before it can run its programs, it needs to receive the instructions. Programming comes directly from the conscious mind. The superconscious mind is our best friend. The superconscious mind does not argue with us when we ask it for help. It simply awaits your instructions, and when it gets those instructions, it puts them into action.

Talking to our superconscious is a bit like writing a letter to self. It is not necessary to put it onto paper but putting it on paper will remind our conscious mind what it is that we have been asking for. It's hard to believe that we can forget what your prayers are, but when we stop and think how often we change your mind, it is little wonder that the superconscious mind has been programmed to beware of this. It knows that the personality is confused to what it wants and is fickle. It understands more about us than we understand about ourselves, because it is closer to our soul than the personality is. When we repeat a request with conviction and honesty, and the request is not out of line with our spirit, then the superconscious mind will grant our requests. Our requests must be reasonable. There would be no reason to grant a request such as being able to lift a building.

People make unreasonable requests every day. A request for millions of dollars is not necessarily a reasonable request from our spirit. People have told me that they have constantly asked the Universe for abundance of money, and then they continue to receive the same amount of money or even less. They wonder what they're doing wrong. We can't sit in a meditative position and expect money to fall out of the sky. People are doing just that. Unless we are a master at manifesting, we will need to take action to create new avenues for money. It does our spirit no justice if people are giving us money we do not need. They might feel sorry for us, and are enabling us, but they are doing us a disservice. They may be thwarting an opportunity for self-growth required by the soul's directives. Pity is not a function of the superconscious mind. However, it does have mercy, and it wants us to have all the things that we truly desire. If we desire things that are detrimental to others, our superconscious will not cooperate.

Another concern about asking for a million dollars is that the money may not be useful to plans to fulfill the soul's directives. It could also be that the soul has a better plan to achieve the attributes we think can only come from money. For example, freedom, joy, ease, and empowerment may be found in aligning with our soul's passions or the companionship of inspiring people. It is best to be specific results when asking our superconscious mind for something.

There should be no doubt that our requests are reasonable. One way to remove doubts is to ask the superconscious mind to remove any discordant programs. Discordant programs consist of many things, emotions, memories or beliefs that tend to repeat in the mind. We may think we're fat, and because of this belief maybe we always will be. We may think we'll never find a better job. We may think we'll never make friends. These are all examples of discordant programs that may be holding us back from achieving our goals. Discordant programs can also include information that is picked up by the subconscious mind. For example, if something tragic happened to us, a minor detail not directly associated with the tragedy it may later trigger delayed emotional response. It may have been raining the day the tragedy occurred, causing us now to feel anxiety on rainy days. These hidden subconscious programs can hinder our manifestations.

The biggest discordances that run in our subconscious mind, that hinders our growth, are discordant programs that other people have unconsciously put there. A good example of a discordant program is when parents teach a child what is real in the world and what is not, and their own prejudices often come out in the children then we know that the child is only playing out what he or she has learned. These prejudices can limit the positive human experiences of the child.

We also tend to take negative comments or insults personally. Those negative comments can be stored in the subconscious mind as potentially useful information. If someone tells you that you are an idiot, the superconscious mind will not filter out the comment if the conscious mind agrees. It will send it to the subconscious mind for processing. The subconscious mind does not know if this is a true statement. It will keep it there until it is processed by the subconscious mind. These discordant programs, which consist of beliefs as well as gained information from the cultural up-bringing, will continue to operate until we successfully eliminate them. The subconscious mind will store programs that are the result of your current life experiences. We can remove it by requesting the superconscious mind to delete the discordant program. We can even request that the superconscious mind remove all self-limiting discordant programs without us even consciously knowing what they are.

There have been many attempts to teach humans to use the power of the superconscious mind. Jesus taught us to pray to God. It was an easy thing to teach, and our ancestors did not have terminology that society has today. In effect, Jesus taught humanity a method of communicating to the superconscious mind, though he did not refer to it as such. "Ask and you shall receive," was a good way to convey needs and to put the request for change out there. Jesus also had many teachings that helped individuals overcome doubt—in effect, getting rid of discordant programs—and demonstrated that in the Universe miracles can happen.

Here is a step-by-step method of talking to our superconscious mind about a desire we want to manifest. When we talk to our superconscious mind, our spirit guides will also hear us and assist.

1) Eliminate the internal chatter. The conscious mind is jam-packed full of thoughts. You would not expect the spirit guides to have to filter through the chaff to hear a specific request. If you are filled with doubt about whether your request to the spirit world is reasonable then the superconscious mind will not act on it. If you find yourself thinking about something other than the request, then repeat it over and over. Do this every day and the chances will increase exponentially that we will be heard. We can also write your requests down to help you keep focused.
2) Let go of feelings that are doubtful or negative. Affirmations that are positive in nature can override the negative thoughts but it is still a good idea to catch yourself every time you have and a negative thought and say," Cancel, clear that last thought." Ask your superconscious mind to remove discordant programs that may negate your request. In addition, you can scan your conscious beliefs to see which ones may be blocking you from achieving your goals and think of ways to dissolve their strength. Seek the help of others that are positive and inspiring if needed, to get rid of distorted negative beliefs.
3) Write positive scripts down on a piece of paper about your desire. The guides will hear your thoughts easily and writing it down helps to validate your ideas to the entire Universe.
4) Say to the superconscious mind, "I would like your help. This is what I want." It is like a prayer in that regard, and it is important to let the spirit world know that it may begin now. You can end the prayer with something like, "Amen" or, "So be it", but anything to let the superconscious mind know that you are ready to get to work on it and begin receiving.
5) Fear is what keeps you from getting what you want, and doubt builds fear. If you are afraid that you do not deserve to get the request fulfilled, the superconscious mind will give you more of what you are expecting. There is no request that is too little or too big to ask for, if it is reasonable.

Jesus once said, "See that you will not be troubled." Here is a great exercise: ask your superconscious mind:

1) "See that I not be troubled by anger."
2) "See that I not be troubled by fear."

3) "See that I not be troubled by the unknown."
4) "See that I not be troubled by jealousy."
5) "See that I not be troubled by hatred."

Are you starting to get the picture? Jesus was asking you to say this prayer to the superconscious mind so that you wouldn't be bothered by these things. Of course, they didn't have the term 'superconscious mind' in his day.

I have heard the argument that the Universe does not understand the words 'no' or 'not'. Nothing could be further from the truth according to my guides. They told me that we have understood the word no since we were babies. Our superconscious mind understands these words and so does the soul. Jesus said the first step in praying is to say what you do not want followed by asking for what you desire. By praying this way, the ability to manifest could triple.

Here is another, even more powerful request to the superconscious. In this example, you are not using the word 'not.' It may be less confusing to those who are troubled by use of the word *not*.

1) "See that I move into love."
2) "See that I experience prosperity."
3) "See that I move into creativity."
4) "See that my life becomes more meaningful."
5) "See that I leave my legacy behind."

A superconscious request is, effectively, a prayer. However, religious people may think they're speaking to God or Jesus when they pray; they might just be communicating to their superconscious mind. This is why thought alone is efficient enough to come closer to manifesting your desires; it's only between you and your superconscious. Some prayers have little effect. For example, a prayer may not work as well if it is directed at something that is unimportant. Your superconscious hears your requests, and then relays them to the spirit world for processing into manifestations.

Manifestations are a broad term for any requests the spirit world brings us. For Example, if we pray for a healthier body and our body becomes healthier, that would be a manifestation. Manifestations are effectively blessings from the spirit world, and are granted based on the seriousness of the request or whether the request is in line with the spirit's best interests.

If the conscious mind desires something that the superconscious mind knows is not in the best interest of the soul, the request can be denied. It's important to note that, as you see in the previous chapter, the conscious mind can be fickle. It may ask for an entirely different experience the following day. The truth is the superconscious mind knows what is best for the spirit. If the conscious mind repeats the request and it is in the best interest of the spirit, the request is taken much more seriously.

Know that we must be specific and focused when we make these requests if we ever hope to make them work. I know people who have told me that prayer does not work for them. For example, I've met plenty who claim they pray all the time about being healthier. However, in these cases, I often find that they are either not specific about their requests—often simply saying 'healthier' without explaining in more detail—or they are simply being vain—that they want to be skinnier or better-looking. Being skinnier alone doesn't make you healthier. However, if they say they're having blood sugar problems and they want a healthy pancreas, the superconscious mind will get to work on that.

For example, I know someone who wanted to look specifically like someone else. They prayed for this specific request for years; when I saw them after that time, I discovered they had in fact come to look closer to their desired person. The difference was amazing; we wouldn't have recognized the person from their previous self.

Our physical appearance can be changed by our own desires, although it is a gradual process. People who desire to become more attractive or more intelligent can ask the superconscious mind to assist. The superconscious can process the communication or request in one of many ways. It can alert the Master Creator of the desire and send the processing factors to the subconscious mind to help create the new reality.

Perhaps we have asked for something that did not come to fruition and we're frustrated as to why that might be. It may be a case where we may have to change the soul contract in order to turn an unmanifested prayer into a manifested prayer. The prayer will then become effective because we have changed the polarity in such a way to repel things that are not in our best interest and attract things that are in harmony with our revised soul contract.

Some unmanifested prayers are just simply prayers that have not properly aligned themselves yet. They will eventually manifest, but we may need more patience. Here is a good example: someone has asked that they find a partner in their life. They may have been dating for years yet none of the people they have met seem to be symbiotic with them. The Universe may be bringing them a person that will be the perfect partner, but the proximity of the person that you may attempt to manifest could be at a

Chapter 16 – The Superconscious Mind

distance. The Universe is in the process of setting up conditions so that we will cross paths, but if we ignore our intuitive process, then we're delaying or even derailing that opportunity. In chapter 20, we will learn ways to improve our intuition.

Removing Discordant Programs

To get rid of a discordant program, pay close attention to yourself over the day. First, concentrate on the things you tell yourself, the things that bother you or keep you up at night. What are those things? Take out a sheet of paper and make your list. Do you find that any of these feel-like broken records? Do they simply repeat without connection to other thoughts? These are very likely examples of discordant programs. When you have isolated what specifically is repeating, pray to your superconscious to get rid of these programs. It may feel counter-intuitive to put even more thought into something is consuming so much of your mind already. Over time, you find yourself thinking less and less about these programs.

A trapped emotion is nothing more than a discordant program with the difference being that it builds up energetically in the body. It is just destructive energy, and we may not even be aware that we are carrying this. Trapped emotions occur when our mind has not been able to process an emotional occurrence. Furthermore, they can even be inherited from past generations. These trapped emotions exist in an energetic layer in our body affecting us physically, mentally, emotionally, and spiritually. These trapped emotions that we aren't aware of can be easily removed.

There are many ways to release trapped emotions, but the best way I've found is to stimulate the nervous system on the back with touch therapy. I do this at the end of every healing. If the guides recognize that someone is carrying a lot of trapped emotional energy, they usually have me put one finger on each side of the spinal cord and stroke down three times. By stroking down three times on each side of the body, we release the energy that bonds the trapped emotions. Then we stroke down the arms three times. Finally, move to the head and stroke from the back of the head to the base of the neck. The person need not be aware that we are releasing trapped emotions.

If one wants to release trapped emotions and they convey this to us then I can tell them exactly what trapped emotion I am removing. For instance, if a person is having a great deal of difficulty with grief, I may ask them to rate their level of grief on a scale from one to ten. The number one would represent hardly any grief, and ten would represent an enormous amount of grief. Then I use the procedure to release a trapped emotion. Some people prefer to use magnets to help pull the energy, the trapped emotion, out of the electro-magnetic field. My guides say they don't need me to use magnets, but if one is available, it can be helpful for others. Once we have released a trapped emotion, one can be quizzed to find out how they feel about the emotion by using the same scale from one to ten.. If a person seems to have no attachment to the emotion anymore, then we are done. If they still find that there is still some grief, we can repeat the process. This is enormously beneficial in healing, and I use it on nearly every person that I work with.

In addition, I use the term 'discordant program' to refer to anything that is interfering with the normal process of healing. Geopathic disturbances or perverse energies, that get into the physical body and attaches itself into the electrical or spiritual body, are a form of discordant programs and others commonly refer to them as perverse energies. I think this is essentially the same thing. These disturbances can be caused by unnatural or natural sources, although the unnatural sources tend to be the most damaging. Radiation from electronic equipment is a good example of an unnatural source that causes an electrical disturbance in the body that can even damage your cell structure. Radiation from the sun is an example of a natural source that also can cause damage to the cell structure—especially on the skin.

There are many techniques that will protect us from geopathic disturbances. For example, our clothing can protect us from the sun's radiation effects such as those effects from prolonged exposure. A healer can remove energies from the electrical body by doing touch or massage. However, the skin may have already been damaged from too much Sun so don't think that healing is going to turn redness to tan. What we are working on is the person's energy body. The energy that is being sent through a person's hands is coming from a source that is outside their own physical body. It is directed by our spirit guides and sent through the healer to assist another, so in a sense a healer is the conduit through which healing occurs.

Our mind is also effective at creating invisible shields to protect us from disturbing energies. We can ask our superconscious mind to build a shield around our body to protect from harm from these energies. For example, traveling in an airplane can cause our body to absorb a high amount of perverse energy. Being around a lot of electrical equipment like computers, cell phones, or televisions, can transmit perverse electrical energy into our body. In both cases, we may request that the superconscious mind shield us from the negative energies. There is little reason for the

Chapter 16 – The Superconscious Mind

superconscious mind to deny that request. Still, I rarely find anyone who understands that they have this ability. It is true especially if they do not understand the concept of the superconscious mind.

I will give you a quick exercise. Imagine a white light surrounding and protecting you. Feel the warmth of the white light and allow it to penetrate every cell in your body. Once you have sat with this for a few minutes imagine the energy field around you. How are you changing it? If you could then photograph your energy field, you would be surprised how identical it would appear to be as to what you imagined. Currently, we have not developed a sophisticated enough technology to photograph all of the energies of the Universe. At some point in the future, the technology will advance, and people will begin using their minds in ways that they have not even thought of.

It is possible to create physical structures with the power of our mind. It is first necessary to remove any discordant programs such as doubt. Doubt is a big one; doubt can prevent you from using the power of our mind. It makes sense that, if our conscious mind doesn't believe in us, then it's derailing the removal of discordant programs. This is one reason we rely on others to help us with our healing. We trust them more than we trust ourselves.

Even in the Biblical days, the clergy understood that discordant programs could be removed, and they used water as a way to magnify the energetic removal of discordant programs. Eventually the technique became symbolic as a baptism. I like to use the power of a shower at the end of the day to remove energies that I may have collected unconsciously. A shower combined with positive intent is an effective way of removing discordant programs on our own. People often report that they sleep better after they've showered. This is largely since energies that are disturbing to our electrical field are magically shed.

Whatever method we use to remove a discordant program, it is not as important as it is to be consistent. With all the perverse energies in our environment today, it would be wise to consciously remove all discordant programs by using the power of the superconscious mind. We can simply say, "Superconscious mind, after we're done running priority programs, please remove all discordant programs and shield me from any perverse energies. So be it."

The Indirect Prayer

An indirect prayer is any energy that attracts to us for some reason but that our conscious mind may not understand. What type of energies do you attract? Some people attract negative people and difficult situations into their life to help them grow and complete their soul contracts. In these cases, a person may appear to be an enemy when they really might be an ally who is here to help you learn a lesson. The Universe will keep sending us the same lesson repeatedly, until we understand and grow beyond it.

I have met people who seem to attract the same type of relationships into their lives and they are frustrated as to why this is occurring. This is a good example of an indirect prayer.

An indirect prayer might be any number of difficulties like a disease, a relationship conflict, a financial setback, or a death in the family. In these situations, problems will not be so easily undone. Instead of the problem correcting itself, we may be inclined to deal with the situation repeatedly. In order to be healed of a specific disease, we might find a strong desire to eat differently, or to travel to another region. Alternatively, we might even be prompted to change the work environment or even the friends that we have. If we do not cooperate with these promptings or we may not experience any positive changes. It is important that we prove to the superconscious mind, and therefore to the spirit world at large, that we indeed want what we request.

I have experienced this firsthand when I was farming, even though it wasn't in my spirit's best interests to farm. I got a lung ailment from the grain dust; when I visited a doctor about it, he said I had to quit or I wouldn't live much longer. At first, I was afraid of making a change in my occupation, but I discovered in a short time that there was life after farming. Eventually I got into something that was more in alignment with my spirit and my lung ailment went away.

Ego, Super-Ego, and Illogism

The superconscious mind contains many components. This includes the Ego, Super-Ego, and Illogism, plus many other complexities and components. The Ego, Super-Ego and Illogism make up twelve percent of the superconscious mind.

The Ego is a Latin word used by Sigmund Freud to refer to self or identity. Ego is not a portion of the soul but a component of the superconscious mind, which is a part of the spirit. The Ego's function is to

Chapter 16 – The Superconscious Mind

find the balance between the primitive drives and the supernatural world and all things in between. Its main function is therefore more of a balancing mechanism. The Ego tends to mediate between the Super-Ego and the Illogism. It is the organized part of the personality that includes, perceptual, intellectual and cognitive functions as well as defensive and executive command functions. It is also responsible for the functions of judgment, emotional control, tolerance, and memory. As once thought, our brain is not the storehouse of memory. The superconscious mind is the part that contains all the memory of past and present experiences. The Ego contains most of the memory functions.

The Illogism is the instinctual interaction that plays a role in moral behavior and critical thinking.

The Super-Ego, unlike Sigmund Freud's description, is an elevated ideal about us that interacts with beings from all dimensions and our soul. It is a super-analytical aspect of the superconscious mind that goes beyond the Ego's critical thinking.

When a person is out of balance, they can become overly primal (too much Illogism) or what society calls egotistical (too much Super-Ego). Having a large Ego has been compared to having an extremely high opinion of oneself and one's purpose in life. I hear people use this term incorrectly all the time. It would be more accurate to say that someone has an over-inflated Super-Ego.

The Illogism drives the Ego but it does not control the Ego. For instance, the Illogism has no judgment about our struggles and external anxieties such as theft, murder, and invasion. The emotional responses of the Illogism are neutral. The Ego in contrast might be repulsed by theft, murder and invasion. The Ego keeps us in check when it comes to staying in alignment with our ethics and morals. Humility is often mistaken as absence of Ego, when in truth; it is a balanced Ego, Super-Ego and Illogism.

The Super-Ego has supernatural forces acting upon it. The strength of the forces acting on the Super-Ego has an impact on the Ego but the Ego seems to be more loyal to the Illogism, preferring to gloss over the finer details of our lives to minimize its conflicts. It is the Super-Ego that constantly watches all the Ego's moves and affects the Ego with feelings of guilt and inferiority. To overcome this, the Ego extracts from the Illogism all of its defense mechanisms. These defense mechanisms are described as morals, taboos, and cultural expectations (allowing the Ego to override the Super-Ego's standards with society's standards). It is the Ego that rationalizes right from wrong by drawing from the Illogism and the Super-

Ego. An inflated sense of one's self-worth is therefore not a product of the Illogism.

There are many other components in the superconscious mind other than the Ego, Super-Ego and the Illogism as the superconscious is so vast and complex that it precedes modern day definition.

Now that you have a better understanding of how our superconscious mind functions, we can begin to sense the sheer power we have within us. Without knowledge of our superconscious mind, we might easily pass the responsibility for our own misgivings to something like genetics, environment, or bad luck. That is simply not the case; we are responsible for our own health and wellbeing. Knowing that we have a superconscious mind is a huge step toward assuming control of our body and our lives. The next step is to use the knowledge that we have gained to take back control of our superconscious mind instead of it just running with the limiting programs our society has given us.

The superconscious is the part of the mind that seems to have the strength to create miracles. It is not there only for survival of the human body but to make us as comfortable as it can. It doesn't matter whether we talk to our superconscious mind through prayer, through affirmations, through positive thinking. It is only important that we talk to and send requests to the superconscious mind. Ask and we shall receive.

Chapter 17 – The Subconscious Mind

We have learned that the conscious mind is the part of us that interacts with the physical realm, and the superconscious mind is the part that connects our physical self to the spiritual world. The third mind—the subconscious mind—serves two main functions. It is responsible to record impartially our interactions and experiences, and two; it sends us messages on what our conscious mind needs to work on for its spiritual growth. In general, our subconscious mind stores memories away mainly to help us later in life. It typically remembers what is relevant to our current life. However, some of the memories may have distorted our beliefs that have we such as acting, feeling, and believing irrationally.

Unlike our physical brain, which works with our conscious mind to access any details from our lives that are stored in our souls, the subconscious mind only receives and stores what the superconscious mind deems the most important information for our lives in general. This information includes what we need for our spiritual development and what our conscious mind believes to be true about us. Our superconscious will usually filter out any data that is not the truth but sometimes these things slip into the subconscious mind.

For example, say at some point someone we were trying to be accepted or loved by, told us that they thought we were ugly. Our superconscious mind may not send this message to the subconscious unless the conscious mind accepts it as the truth. If the conscious mind is undecided about the truth of a particular statement, the superconscious may still forward it to the subconscious if it deems the conscious mind needs to learn from this. The subconscious can then send the conscious mind help to resolve the problem. The superconscious mind knows what is best for us even though we think the data is damaging. Perhaps we need to build up our self-esteem and accept what we look like or build a firmer back bone to not let other's opinions sway our opinions of who we are and what we think we look like. Then again, perhaps our appearance could use some improvement for the work we need to be doing. The subconscious will direct the conscious mind to the situation. If the conscious mind does not grow beyond the issue, anyone who implies we are ugly will add fuel to the fire since the belief is now stored in the subconscious.

The subconscious mind receives directives from the superconscious mind such as what the soul wants the conscious mind to achieve. The soul's directives could be concerning many areas of our lives including, career, family, mental and physical health, and other areas of our lives. The subconscious mind relays this information through a variety of mechanisms. The subconscious mind doesn't store just negative emotions and beliefs; it also stores positive ones. It might be helpful to have a few negative beliefs about ourselves to keep a sense of humility. A person can become too egotistical if too overloaded with positive feedback. For example, famous people sometimes become delusional about how great they are due to many people fanning their super-ego. This is how the expression fan came into being. Having a strong opinion about who we are is not a problem to the spirit. It only becomes a problem if the person cannot remain humble.

The subconscious mind is in a sense the quarantine zone. It can be a repository for socially unacceptable ideas, wishes, or desires. In addition, it can be a great place to store painful emotions that formulated in the conscious mind. The subconscious mind can be accessed and reviewed, but it is set apart from your conscious mind so that it does not continue to interfere with everyday life.

Since I am presenting a basic overview of the subconscious, I will not expand on other functions it has other than a bit about how it reinterprets data to send to the conscious mind.

So, what does the subconscious mind have to do with the dream state? Dreams are messages from our collective experience that are filtered through the subconscious to make sense of what we are experiencing in your lives. We are not always consciously aware what the spirit's objectives are. The superconscious mind, on the other hand, does understand what our missions are and sends this information to the subconscious mind. The understanding of our mission and things we want to work on in this lifetime are stored deep in the subconscious mind along with all of our unresolved emotional issues. The subconscious determines what needs to be addressed to the conscious mind in the dream state. It is just as important to dream, as it is to sleep. Not everyone remembers their dreams consciously, but dreams are still processed. Repetitive dreams are ones that are looking for resolve.

Each dream can have a unique message. The messages from our dreams may not always be interpreted by the conscious mind to the extent that we can write about it, but we do act on our dreams without really thinking. It is an automatic process so therefore it is immaterial in many cases if the conscious mind remembers the dream. Dreams are just one small avenue that our subconscious must help accomplish our soul's directives. To understand our dreams better, we may need to review our dreams in the conscious mind. Sometimes this is why we remember some dreams better than others do. A dream can be piped from the subconscious into our conscious mind.

The nice part about dreams is that there is no one else interfering in the dream process. The interpretations and understandings of our dreams are our own. If we decide to ask someone else about their interpretation of our dream, it can influence our conscious interpretation, but has no bearing on the superconscious interpretation. If the superconscious believes that the dream has adequately resolved some issue, then it removes the dream from the subconscious mind. Only the superconscious can do this.

The subconscious uses three bodies to process data. This includes the mental body, the emotional body and the physical body. These bodies are energies that envelope our aura. The aura is the energetic glow that surrounds our physical body. The mental body stores higher intellectual data and is partially responsible for memory. People, who have a strong connection to their mental body, live in an organized fashion. Traumas can weaken our connection to the mental body. This is not helpful if the person needs to heal from the trauma.

The emotional body stores all the emotions that have occurred and scales them as to their importance. For example, if the emotional body thinks loneliness is the most important, it moves it to the #1 position for our subconscious to send to our conscious mind to work on. The subconscious also reinterprets messages from the physical body if a specific part needs healing. It will send a message to the conscious mind that a physical ailment needs repair. The conscious mind then transmits the information to the superconscious mind that draws in healing energy from the Universe. If the superconscious cannot immediately heal a problem energetically, it will attract things into the person's life to get the conscious mind to create an action of some sort that assists with healing.

Clearing Your Subconscious

We have heard how the subconscious mind will store negative information. There are countless techniques used by psychologists and others to clear the subconscious mind of negative, trapped emotions.

Phobias are good examples of how negative trapped emotions can interfere with our happiness. We may want to clear them from our subconscious. If we have great dream recall, it may be an indication that our subconscious mind is clearing trapped emotions. Dreams do a good clearing some negative emotions but not all of them. In the absence conscious interface, these negative emotions are still left in the subconscious mind and the clearing process not entirely effective so we can assist the body if we understand how the process works.

As mentioned before, my spirit guides have taught me a simple technique to use at the end of a healing. The person receiving the healing does not even have to be consciously aware that we are removing negative trapped emotions from them. We can ask a person specifically if they would like to remove negative trapped emotions. Again, this technique greatly enhances the effect of the healing, and removes a lot of negative energy.

You should note: The subconscious mind's purpose is to store emotions—both positive and negative. It is not necessarily improper to have emotions stored in the subconscious. However, too many negative emotions or emotions that have been trapped can clog the mind and interfere with everyday living. Our motivations of why we believe, feel, or act the way we do can be driven by beliefs coming from the subconscious mind that we are not even aware of.

Our subconscious mind can and should be a great ally in achieving success in our lives. First, we need to know what it does before we decide to clean out all the files. There could be some useful information that we may not want to lose.

Some of our most creative thoughts stem from processing the information in our subconscious mind. When in the suneidesis conscious state; artists, musicians, and professionals, draw information from the subconscious to make ideas flow more smoothly. The subconscious stores memories of past mistakes so we will not make them again.

When I am making new music, I am establishing a working relationship with my subconscious mind. I remember what chord progressions make sense and which chords don't fit together and then I practice that piece repeatedly. When it becomes so automatic, people can play a music piece without even thinking about it. The hands will develop muscle memory and they will automatically perform so our conscious mind gets out of the way.

Our subconscious mind likes repetition, and the more we perform a piece, the easier the piece will be. If we come back to play a piece of music that we have not performed for many years, much of the muscle memory is gone and we will have to focus more with our conscious mind. The minute we focus the conscious mind, a new file will be created. The old file is still there but it is harder to bring up. If we can just let our subconscious mind get back into the flow, we will not have to rememorize the piece of music all over again, but if we allow our conscious mind to think that we need to relearn the music then it will take more time and effort to start the process over again. If we were to play the piece from time to time, the memory will stay nearer to the surface and will stay automatic. If we never practice the song after first learning it, the subconscious mind does not think it is pertinent and the file can become buried.

The Subconscious/Superconscious Relationship

Our subconscious mind does not act upon any request or instruction sent directly from our conscious. The subconscious mind only reacts to instructions that come from our superconscious mind. If we are repetitively telling our superconscious mind something, it is relayed to the subconscious mind.

The subconscious mind is constantly sending us data that we need when experiencing new conscious events. It ties our new experiences to previous ones, comparing them in the process. The subconscious is sending us data, but it only gets this information from the superconscious mind. The superconscious mind determines what to send and what to filter out. Not all information is pertinent to store in the subconscious. It doesn't care where the computer is, how the living room is arranged, how cluttered the home is. Instead, it stores pertinent data about life choices, and the consequences of those choices.

Negative Trapped Emotions

There are times when the subconscious mind's clutter can become problematic. Sometimes siblings will harass the other by telling them they are stupid. Since the subconscious mind and the superconscious mind have no judgment about the saying, it may record it as a fact. In this case, it would be wise to deprogram those thoughts and if we have any of these programs running, we should ask our superconscious mind to 'cancel, clear' any of those programs. We should clear any programs that are not in our highest interest.

Unwanted emotions and experiences can get stored in the subconscious mind. However, these emotions can be released from the emotional body, which is attached to our central nervous system. We call them trapped emotions, but they are not really trapped. They are held up but for the most part, they work their way out automatically. If they seem to be trapped it means they haven't had the proper opportunity to work them out. They will move out either in the dream state or by interactions with others. If these emotions build, they can become detrimental to our mental state and our physical health. The trapped emotions cannot only distort our beliefs, causing havoc in our lives, but they can also attract similar traumas to occur. In this case, it would be better to ask the superconscious mind to release the negative trapped emotions. There would be no reason to release any of the positive emotions that can contribute to the joy of living. The more we practice positive affirmations, the less likely, that any negative ones will supersede them.

When I am doing a healing on a person, I often find that there is enormous emotional baggage. This is just another way to refer to negative trapped emotions. We hear this term frequently, but we are unaware of how to clear emotional baggage. I picture in my mind that I am taking out the garbage. This garbage is energetic but is as real as physical garbage. To remove emotional baggage, I use a similar technique as described previously of standing behind a person and wiping my hands in a downward motion from their neck to the base of their pelvis. I do these motions three times, and then I swipe along the sides of the body three times, down the arms, from the top of the head, and down off the shoulders. I can inform them that I am removing a negative trapped emotion, but in some cases, I don't even need to mention that I am doing that. While I am in this process, I am using my own positive affirmation—something we should do too if we attempt to remove negative trapped emotions. We can say these affirmations aloud, or to ourselves; it makes no difference.

Here are three common phrases I use in releasing trapped emotions:

1) "We are getting rid of the emotion of ____" (Here, you would name the specific emotion plaguing the person.)
2) "It doesn't serve you any purpose... it is not a part of who you are."
3) "You can release it now... just let it go."

Using these three phrases can significantly help remove these trapped emotions. In some cases, we might even find it valuable to have the person say these phrases with you.

Positive Affirmations

The subconscious cannot distinguish between what is real and what is imaginary. This is why visualizations, affirmations and repeated images can have such a powerful effect in our lives. We can also do exercises to create images within ourselves that are nourishing to the subconscious mind. Positive affirmations work best when done every day because the subconscious mind likes repetition. In addition, what we focus our attention on will attract more of it into our lives.

Have a personal discussion and decide on the specific qualities we like or want in ourselves. If we can isolate these specifics, we can form them into affirmations. Simply tell yourself "I am—" followed by whatever quality you strive for.

If we can't decide on what specific affirmation, we want to say to ourselves, we may also say these following general affirmations:

1) "I am of Love."
2) "I am capable, intelligent, and talented."
3) "I have a lot to offer the world."
4) "The Universe is loving and helpful, my needs are always met."

Say either our own affirmations or these suggested ones at least once daily. Incorporating them into daily routine will help reinforce so we don't forget to do it. We can use this as part of your morning ritual, before a meal, or as a prayer before we go to sleep.

If we find ourselves fishing for compliments, it may be time to start doing daily affirmations. Others can tell you we're smart, beautiful, or handsome, but we won't necessarily internalize the qualities into our subconscious mind until we begin affirming them. What matters most is how we see ourselves. Have you ever heard someone say, "Coming from you, that compliment means a lot"? That is because they value your own opinion more than someone else's opinion. However, what it boils down to is that we value our own opinions the most. We need to give ourselves compliments, instead of fishing for them from others.

I have a hard time giving myself compliments and many people do. People waste a lot of time fishing for compliments from others, especially if they are storing a lot of negative information from their past. Some parents are not good at recognizing that children need to fill their subconscious mind with positive information. This is the main reason that it is important to not be overcritical of someone else. Whether they are young children or not, makes no difference, but the fact remains that all people need some validation.

Don't forget that *negative* affirmations can be dangerous just as positive affirmations can be helpful. If we wake up every morning and fret about how we don't like something about our body, how we've aged, how worthless we are—these are still a form of daily affirmation. However, we're affirming the negative qualities in our lives, potentially qualities that aren't even true.

One of the worst affirmations I've heard from people is, "It's hell to live to be this old." This is just setting us up for expectations that old age is going to be painful.

Chapter 18 – Above the Three Minds

We have now learned how about the three minds. Our conscious mind collects the physical data from the world around us. Our superconscious mind takes the direct experiences from our conscious mind and records that information at the soul level while sending pertinent information to the subconscious mind for storage. When needed, our subconscious pulls previous memories forth, allowing us to best navigate our lives. These three minds may work independently from each other at times, but when they work together, we can become more spiritually developed.

Conscious Interface

The conscious interface is a process of how the three minds work. Our conscious mind connects us to our superconscious mind. Our superconscious mind sends information to our subconscious mind—not the other way around. People may think they can communicate with their subconscious mind; when they're communicating with the superconscious mind. When the superconscious mind gets information, it can store it in the subconscious mind. Our conscious thoughts are heard by our superconscious mind. If we think the same thoughts repeatedly, the superconscious may store that information in the subconscious mind.

Here is how the conscious interface works. The conscious mind sends instructions to the superconscious mind. The superconscious mind sends those instructions to the subconscious mind. The subconscious mind then carries out those instructions and communicates the information directly to the conscious mind. The full circuit of communication among the three components of the mind is conscious interface.

Messages from the Spirit World

The Three Minds

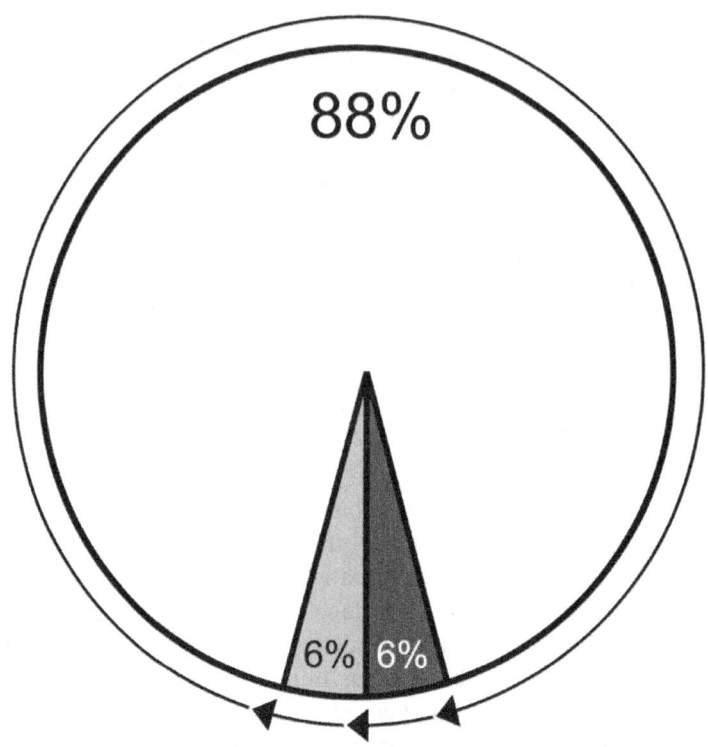

☐ Superconscious Mind
◨ Conscious Mind
■ Subconscious Mind

Chapter 18 – Above the Three Minds

Our subconscious mind communicates someone's feelings, and we might have a conscious thought about a feeling that we once communicated to the superconscious mind. We might have forgotten we even communicated this thought, but since it was stored in the subconscious mind, it comes back into our awareness. When a hypnotherapist begins talking about regressing us into the subconscious mind, what they fail to recognize is that there's first a superconscious mind. The hypnotherapist may not be aware that they are able to talk to the superconscious mind and they might think that they are dealing with the subconscious mind. The misunderstanding can lead to erroneous treatment because we can't treat the two the same. What is stored in the subconscious mind is completely protected and without permission from the superconscious, it will not be accessed.

Therefore, we can see that the conscious interface is in a circular fashion. It does not bounce back and reverse directions. The Universal Creator must have considered that it would be dangerous to remove these safeguards. The more we think about it, the more it makes sense that the conscious interface is how we communicate with our three minds. If this were a random event, with no structure, then our thoughts would always be different every day, and our beliefs would change daily. Without our conscious interface and the way in which each of our three minds work, we would never be able to maintain our personalities and belief systems. The conscious interface is a huge stabilizer for our personality. Our beliefs do not change so easily even when our thoughts do.

The things we accomplish in life—our successes, our challenges—are largely due to the stabilizing effect of conscious interface. We would probably change occupations daily if it weren't for the conscious interface. Our race probably may not have advanced to the point it is now if it were not for the effects of conscious interface. Remember our skill level relies of repetition.

Let us say for instance that we could talk directly to the subconscious mind. What information do you think we would get? Since the subconscious mind is a storehouse, it doesn't have the ability to interpret data to be able to make correct assumptions. It might create irrelevant ideas that the spirits like to call '*bullshit*.' Our subconscious mind could create a mountain of this stuff if it wanted to. However, I don't think it would do anyone any good unless we were considering writing a science fiction novel based on completely irrelevant thoughts.

On the other hand, talking to our superconscious mind is like talking to our soul. The soul is constantly searching for the truth. It doesn't create lies. One of the best things about our superconscious minds is that we can trust it. Our superconscious mind is so chock-full of filters that it does not permit the conscious mind to bullshit it. It can discern whether we are serious about a command or request. This is because it is the direct connection to the soul, and it knows what's best for us.

For example, if our conscious mind decides to commit suicide, it may choose to do so in a variety of ways. Our superconscious mind may influence us toward taking poison, causing a physical reaction of throwing up to keep us alive. It is not in our best interest for our physical bodies to die, even though our conscious mind may think it is a good idea. Our conscious thoughts are not always the purest, so we can thank the Universal Creator for giving us a superconscious mind, so we don't act on improper conscious thoughts. For the most part, our superconscious mind is a higher command center.

Conscious interface is necessary for individuals to achieve their goals and desires. The Universe we live in is multifaceted. It uses conscious interface to heal, to create, to manifest, to connect to the Akashic records, and other useful processes.

Conscious interface can help us find the solutions to our problems. The superconscious mind receives information from the conscious mind. The superconscious mind then relays the information to the subconscious mind. If we don't communicate what we want in life to our superconscious mind, then we don't get the things that we desire. Jesus taught, "Ask and you shall receive." He was speaking about the process of conscious interface. Understanding how the three minds work is one of the primary laws that you should understand to live a fulfilling life.

There has been much confusion about the process of conscious interface. There is some confusion about the superconscious versus the subconscious mind. The superconscious mind has a connection to the Akashic records that the subconscious mind does not. The subconscious mind only serves the conscious mind.

The Universal Mind

We now understand the way the three minds work for us. Our conscious, superconscious, and subconscious minds work together to gather knowledge and experience. Our three minds form our spirit, which report to the soul on all we have learned and done. However, we may wonder where

Chapter 18 – Above the Three Minds

our knowledge goes after that. How is it that we can share experiences when we each connect to a different soul? The answer is simple: all souls connect automatically to something even bigger—a vast collection of all our memories and experiences. This is the Universal Mind. The Universal Mind contains Akashic records but is much more than that. It contains the records about the Universe, thus the terminology.

The Universal Mind is the only complete source of information in the Universe, but it is not simply some brick-and-mortar library in the heavens. Rather, a living energetic being resides in the celestial realm. It actively collects the experiences from every living being in every galaxy, and every Universe. That means you, your family, your friends, and even your pets are reporting to the Universal Mind. Even species on each planet and each dimension, are sending their experiences to their specific mass consciousness file for their species, which are all contained within the Universal Mind. There are no secrets from the Universal Mind.

Souls can access the shared experiences of other souls through the Universal Mind. This allows souls to grow and develop their understanding of the complexity of the Universe, which in turn advances creation. Without a central stored location of information, creation would become stagnant; our civilizations would be doing the same thing now that they did eons ago. With the Universal Mind, we can retain the advances our ancestors have made. Since this vast wealth of information is available to the soul for the journeys, we do not need to reinvent the wheel.

Spiritual Access of the Universal Mind

Although the Universal Mind is mainly for souls to access, we as spirits can tap into it as well. Though it's not easy, tapping into the Universal Mind can lead to fast learning or quickened wisdom. The most adept of our species has been able to learn a language in a week's time or develop ideas never seen in our history. Great geniuses like Nikola Tesla and Albert Einstein, while intelligent, were able to access their most groundbreaking concepts through direct connection to the Universal Mind. Repeatedly in history, we see this happen; when a spirit brings forward ideas or technologies that hadn't been conceived before, we can bet that their great minds were assisted by the Universal Mind, either from direct access by their soul or indirectly from their spirit guides.

Tapping into the information of the Universal Mind is not new, but it is not common to do. It is not like tapping into our own superconscious; this is the encyclopedia of encyclopedias we are trying to access. In fact, we see it is quite rare to find someone else who knows anything about the Universal Mind, much less know how to tap into it. Still, it is possible. Accessing the Universal Mind has been taught by advanced beings in the past, and a few spirits are still capable of accessing it today.

In the past, people who could most easily access the Universal Mind were called *disciples*. There have been disciples in all religions. As we might expect, a *disciple* has developed strong spiritual discipline. Nowadays, we refer to those people as master teachers. Spiritual discipline can be achieved by integrating the three minds, the conscious, the subconscious and the superconscious, reaching the point of conscious interface. We do not have to be master teachers to do this effectively. Anyone can.

Every person has the ability to communicate with the Universal Mind . It can be broken down into different departments, each department relating to a species. These individual departments are sometimes referred to as the Akashic records library. As it stands, there is a specific Akashic record of earthly humankind within the Universal Mind. The Akashic records are really a storehouse of the information compiled by a species. Each species has its own Akashic library. All the libraries combined get fed into the Universal Mind.

One technique to tap into the Akashic records library is to retrain the brain to simultaneously collect data from the right and the left hemisphere of the brain. Doing this is called 'light speed learning,' and it provides you with a direct connection to the Universal Mind. This is no easy task. There is a whole field of study on how to do it. One of Earth's master teachers, Thomas Morton, taught this method. He created a study program called "Light Speed Learning." It can be used as a valuable tool to access information that is held in the Universal Mind.

Other master teachers have created methods of tapping into the Universal Mind. Spiritual gurus of India have often been associated with tapping into the Universal Mind. Paramahansa Yogananda, in his book *Autobiography of a Yogi*, describes his supernatural experiences. These supernatural experiences often involved connecting to the Universal Mind.

I have met someone who has been gifted with the ability to communicate with animals and many other advanced beings due to her connection to the Universal Mind. She has developed a permanent connection with the Universal Mind and can access information at will. It has been estimated that the number of individuals on Earth that can tap it are roughly 100,000. However, this is an extremely small percentage of the population. These abilities are innate and for humankind to advance, many

Chapter 18 – Above the Three Minds

more individuals must study from the master teachers to learn the ways. By tapping the information of the Universal Mind, humankind can evolve more quickly.

The Essenes had created the *Dead Sea Scrolls* to be found during our lifetime to instruct us in this quickening of evolution. However, there are many archeological discoveries to be made that would make the *Dead Sea Scrolls* seem small in comparison. This information will tell us how our past ancestors accessed the Universal Mind to understand advanced information about the galaxies that our scientists are just beginning to discover.

Some people also can connect to the Universal Mind via their spirit guides. Spirit guides can make it easier for the individual person to access their own information and the information held in the Universal Mind. If an individual cultivates his innate ability to communicate with their spirit guides, then the information becomes accessible.

Since I have an indirect connection to the —as I am connected to my spirit guides, who are connected to the Universal Mind—I have not fostered a more direct connection myself. However, if we feel we need a deeper understanding of the Universe, and cannot connect with our spirit guides, we should look more deeply into connecting to the Universal Mind.

Part 3 – Spiritual Communication

Now that we understand how the mind works, we can use it to communicate with the spiritual world. We do not have to experience the afterlife to communicate with guides, angels or other beings. This section will teach us some basic principles that we can use daily to enrich our lives.

Chapter 19 – Spirit Communication

Spirit communication is the only true form of understanding between individuals. All the languages combined do not have enough words to fully express love for instance. When I think of spirit communication, I think about how animals communicate. Sure, they can make a few sounds but there is something greater than that going on. If we are pet owners, chances are that we have experienced some form of spirit communication.

I had an experience that I will not forget when we were swimming with dolphins while in Cabo, Mexico. I had given a hand signal for a dolphin to place his snout on my hands so I could pose for the photographer. The dolphin swam a few feet and then popped out of the water, looked at me and nodded its head three times. It hit me like a bolt of lightning, that it was saying that I had good energy. Dolphins are known to have a great deal of skill communicating and trainers say that we each have our own unique experiences. He said they send out signals that are impossible to miss. They can teach us a lot if we are willing to pay attention and learn.

Love is something that is felt and our feelings are a form of telepathic understanding. Certainly, the love we have between fellow men is different from the love that we have for a spouse. The love that we have for a spouse is different from the love we have for our children. No matter how angry a parent may be at their children, there is a spirit communication of love passed between individuals. Parents and their children will often find themselves communicating telepathically and are somewhat surprised of the simultaneous transmissions of thought. This often occurs between two friends. With modern day technology, it is easy to see when this occurs. One friend will think of another and within minutes the other friend will call, email or text. This technology is making it easier for the new generation to understand just how powerful spirit communication truly is.

For centuries people have known that negative thought sent to others can result in a backlash effect to the person that sent it. Surprisingly, inanimate objects repel negative thought transmissions back to the sender with even more force than it was sent. This pickup of energy cannot be measured but it is nevertheless significant. The sender of the negative thought may feel as though that they have been struck with an energetic dagger. Thoughts are more powerful than words, for they convey less abstract meaning. Thought conveys cognition, sentience, consciousness and imagination.

Different spiritual disciplines teach that a person must have pure thought in order to achieve optimal health. Pure thought are notions with no negativity. When people are verbalizing their own thoughts, there are often times threads of negativity attached to them, even though the words appear to have no negative connotations. To avoid the incidents of negative connotations, one must ask the superconscious to clear their mind of negativity. This should be done every day and throughout the day. This is an extremely important request to the superconscious and it is quite simple. Now, when two people begin to communicate, if one person has cleared their negative thoughts and the other has not, any negative thoughts during the communication will be returned to the host. This is a strong shield of protection for a person as well.

It is difficult for us to understand the dynamics of likes and dislikes. Most often dislikes are shared negative transmissions of thought. The negative transmissions of thought can create preferences, but those preferences are changeable. For instance, a young person may say they do not like pineapple or fish, and they carry those negative thoughts for many years. These ideas are false. At the time when the young person might have tasted their first pineapple, his natural instincts may have been leading him away from something sweet or sour to something richer in protein. A child may then develop a negative memory that makes them insist that they do not like pineapple. People's needs will change quite quickly; sometimes in as little as a year or sooner.

We do not have to be so close-minded as to allow our negative memories to rule us. We can shed many negative beliefs and obtain new memories to replace the old ones. There is nothing wrong with consuming a pineapple but if we see a pineapple and project our dislike upon it, the energy that is sent into it can become toxic to us. If enough negative thoughts accumulate then these thoughts become a memory that only serves to develop the dislike for pineapple, depriving us of beneficial nutrients. This is a good example of how negative beliefs can lead to deficiencies in health. It is a simple matter of asking our superconscious to shed itself of negative beliefs or dislikes.

What false beliefs have we created? In some cases, the things we think we dislike can actually have miraculous effects on us. In the case of the pineapple, we were influenced to create a negative feeling about it when in fact it might have been good for us.

It is better to ignore opinionated people, especially if those people are extremely persuasive. Opinionated people carry many dislikes wrapped up into a neat package we call a belief. These people project negative understandings onto everyone they encounter. They may believe they are protecting another person from a danger but in fact, they may be damaging the person's ability to make better choices.

Now let us look at the concept of negative backlash. The backlash principle states that those people who advocate principles but do not adhere to them are punishing themselves by being inauthentic. They are sending mixed messages to the superconscious mind and those messages just get recirculated but not processed by the subconscious mind. The information is returned to the conscious mind in a variety of ways. At any rate, the conscious mind can find itself in a quandary. It wants to believe its own teaching but has no intention of acting on its messages. The person will begin to feel guilt, loss of self-worth or become ashamed of its own behavior. Unhealthy does not refer to only the physical state but all states of being the primary state is the emotional state. If we would take the time to notice that the messenger is not necessarily the most likely to follow their own preaching, then we will understand that not all messengers are perfect people.

Negative spirit communications can result in damages to the emotional states of mind. If someone is judging another to be ugly or fat, the other person may begin to feel ugly or fat. This can result in many physical ailments. In many cases, it is the emotional state of mind that needs to be healed first before the physical state of mind can be altered. Medicine treats symptoms but does little to affect what is causing the symptom. Rarely does taking a pill result in a healthier state. There is a psychosomatic effect that does occur when a person ingests a pill, but that effect is just the result of the person directing their superconscious to begin the healing process. The superconscious is responding from the order given by the living host and will often begin the healing process by using the most direct approach. This may not always be desirable. For example, if a host is suffering from a bad heart but is more concerned with a sore muscle elsewhere, the superconscious will direct more of its energy into the sore muscle, thereby ignoring the heart. When a person's body is on autopilot and the heart is the most life-threatening ailment, the host will often get frustrated about a much more trivial matter. For example, a person's appearance is much less important in the end than is the function of the heart. When too much emphasis is placed on the trivial matters, it opens itself to failure. Failure of an organ may result in the death of a host. The superconscious has a preset program that it follows if no other direction is given. It would be better for the host to direct the superconscious to continue to heal the most distressed portion of its body and secondly to heal its appearance. This is a positive and powerful directive that can achieve both objectives in a period. Do not expect outward appearances to change in an instant, for the body has primary concerns to heal first.

When a healer is exchanging energy with a person, they will first direct healing into the astral body where it can affect the primary circuit board of the person's emotions. When the physical body is rewired, they will begin to feel better in an instant. This allows the physical ailments to subside.

When a person is receiving healing, it may be wise to first clear away negative ant thoughts or beliefs. A negative belief about the person administrating the healing may lessen the impact of the healing. These negative thoughts are telepathic transmissions. Secondly, the person receiving the healing should ask their superconscious to allow its spirit guides to conduct a comprehensive healing. Even a skeptic can get a healing. Again, the primary objective is to only allow positive telepathic transmissions. The superconscious wants to achieve one's objectives. It does not matter to the superconscious what the objectives are.

Telepathic transmissions that are used to control another person are much weaker than positive transmissions. This means that negative telepathic transmissions are deficient in energy. If your superconscious is directed to shield itself of all the negative telepathic transmissions, it will do so with ease. Thanking our superconscious is a way to show love for ourselves. Loving ourselves is one of the highest objectives of the divine order. When a person perceives themselves to be inadequate, this negative perception will be stored by the superconscious because it has been directed to do so. To undo this negative perception one has of itself, one must follow the divine order of protocol.

This is the divine protocol:
1 - Love yourself.
2 - Love your neighbor as you love yourself.
3 - Disallow any dislikes to affect you.
4 - Purify your telepathic transmissions.
5 - Calibrate your vibration with the vibration of the Earth.

The key to loving ourselves is to recognize who we are. We cannot recognize who we are unless we eliminate all negative telepathic transmissions about who we are. These transmissions can be sent from others as well as notions that we have about ourselves, and they distort the truth. When more highly evolved beings, eliminate their negative telepathic

Chapter 19 – Spirit Communication

transmissions others perceive them as more attractive. Their positive vibrations emanate in all directions. They develop a personality trait known as charisma.

Charisma carries with it bold responsibilities and golden opportunities, yet some charismatic individuals tend to abuse those privileges. It is an honor to be chosen by the spirit world to relay information of love and truth. When they abuse privileges and turn toward personal gain with no honor in their intentions, then the love and the admiration of those around them will retract. This has resulted in a new identity for the charismatic leader as that of a false prophet. Many false prophets at first emanated their love but then they fell victim to negative spirit communication from others. If this negative spirit communication builds, then anger could erupt leaving them feeling lost and confused. This is how some TV evangelists have fallen victim. The circumstances did not cause the negative telepathic vibrations, nor did an outside external source cause their misfortune. Their misfortune was caused by their unwillingness to communicate with the superconscious and ask help to let go of negative thoughts.

It is easy to forget about asking the superconscious for help. It is much harder to remember to gather one's own wits and follow the protocol of the divine order. When confronted with a disturbing thought or the disturbing action of another, please refer to the protocol of the divine order found earlier in this chapter.

It is important to love our neighbor as we love ourselves. We are all important to God. If we can learn to understand and accept that others may not share our likes and dislikes as their roles may be much different than ours, then we can develop greater tolerance for others. If we turn our anger into loving thoughts, people will view us as a better people. They may understand that our views are much different but if we send loving energy toward them, they will want to know us better.

Some people may have things that they do not like about us. It may just be the clothes that we wear remind them of someone they don't fancy. What people think of us does not describe who we are, but more about who they are and their perceptions of the world. These likes and dislikes are only judgments. We are not a collection of what other people think of us.

It is important to purify our telepathic transmissions. If we are noticing something about someone or something else that disturbs us, we should turn our thoughts to something else that we admire about the person. Alternatively, imagine them enveloped in white light for protection. Surround them with angels. Anything we can do to dissipate the negative telepathic transmissions that we or someone else sent to them can make a positive change.

It is important to calibrate our vibration with the vibration of the Earth. This is actually quite simple to do. Ask that our bodies be given an energetic connection to the Earth that is complimentary. Ask that our body be put into alignment with those frequencies that are harmonious with nature. It is easiest when we are in nature to feel the calibration occur. We may experience a little lightness. Some may notice a shift in their bodies similar to an out of body experience. Any attempt we make to calibrate our energy with the Earth does shift matter.

Imagination

The first step in connecting to the spirit world is to use your imagination. Imagination, in the spiritual sense, is the step above thinking. Thinking is the compilation of data that already exists and using that data in preconceived ways. Imagination, on the other hand, is creating new ways to use the data. Imagination in this context is not just idle chatter; it is thinking about what could be, rather than what is. It is imagining, for example, that you could build a house with Popsicle sticks or something equally outrageous. To conceptualize things that someone else hasn't already achieved, you have to tap into your imagination. Here's the kicker: imagination is a function of the spirit. Your physical brain acts more like a processor so that ideas that lead you to a creative process come from outside your physical body. Your spirit is filled with imagination. Why is that you might ask? According to the spirit world, since your spirit is connected to your soul, and your soul is connected to a source beyond it, your imagination is beyond your conscious mind's understanding. Sometimes these ideas come to us like a lightning bolt strike. We're not sure where this idea came from, it just materialized out of thin air. Every great idea starts with your imagination.

Opening your mind could be considered the most important step, and this requires foresight and telepathic transmission. It is commonplace that too little effort is put into this first step. If you have a desire to connect, you must also have focus. Imagination requires focus, because if you are not clear in your thought process then you may not make that connection.

In order to foster your imagination, you want to get into contact as closely as possible to your own soul. Your spirit is your connection to your soul. Your superconscious mind is your connection to your spirit. Therefore, as you can see, you need to rely on your superconscious mind to help you develop your imagination. Imagination is not automatic. They say when you are in your youngest years you are closest to God, which also happens to be when you have such 'wild' imaginations!

The first step to accessing your imagination is to be clear on what you want to achieve. How can your superconscious mind understand your objectives if you are not clear?

The second step is to ask your superconscious mind to help you create something. This can be anything from an invention to a manifestation.

The third step is to be willing to receive the information. Unbelievably, this is where most people stop their imagination.

Many times, I have asked people whether they have wanted to create something, like an invention. They that they do, but when I ask them what they want to create, they say they don't know. In this case, they have failed the first step; they don't know what they want to achieve. They just want to achieve something, without knowing what it is they want to achieve. According to the spirit world, many people are unimaginative and have a difficult time getting past the first step.

If you pass the first step, and are clear on what you want, you still need to ask your superconscious mind. For example, say a prayer or ask your superconscious mind to help you find the sources to manifest the desire. Then, start listening for leads. Talk to people, do some research, and see where you get led. According to the spirit world, not too many people complete this step either.

Let's say that you have passed the first and second step and are willing to accept the information. The information comes in many ways. It may come from guides, friends, family, media, or a book. Maybe you will see something that will trigger an idea. You need to stay focused on your desire and watch for ideas to come to you. Guides often send their messages through friends and family, so don't discount what others have to say. We can become closed to receiving information from others. This door is closed too often. Sometimes, people even crucify the messenger; they make fun of the information you have.

Many times, the guides have told me that judgments are the root of all evil. How many times have you heard from someone, "That won't work"? They are not even willing to try. This may be partially due to the previous judgments that have developed because of your experiences.

Let's say that you've passed the third step. Now your imagination has kicked into high gear and there's nothing that's going to stop it. Once you have discovered how to open those doorways, you won't go back to our old ways of thinking. Those old ways of thinking no longer serve you. The saying, "thinking outside the box" heard quite often in today's time, implies using your imagination

When you are setting out to create new ideas, the process of imagination, it is important to use an intense focus. After you have completed focusing, you need to communicate your desire telepathically. The result will be much more on target and in line with the spirit guides. Before a connection occurs, it is recommended that you ask the superconscious to clear out all negative thoughts and extraneous ideas that do not apply to the imagination. This will make the procedure of focusing quite a bit easier.

Connecting with your guides is a manifestation technique. It is much the same if you are attempting to connect with angels. It can be difficult to follow through with all the required steps in the imagination process for several reasons. The most common reason is that there is some sort of interference. Interference can be things that divert a person's focus such as, a loud noise, a telephone call or other unwanted distractions. Those things can be sight related, sound related, or energy that is loaded with negativity. A setting with clutter may be enough of a distraction to cancel a person's focus. If there are too many external stimuli present, you may ask the superconscious to shield you from those stimuli. It will place the person into a state that is much more conducive.

For example, an obnoxious jackhammer can interfere with a person's focus and thereby cancel out all notions of a manifestation. An uncomfortable setting or over-sensory stimulation may also cancel out the process of a manifestation. The guides advise that a person get into a comfortable place and block out as much external stimuli as possible.

When there is a loss of vocabulary to describe the manifestation, or the manifestation is difficult to imagine, then it is nearly impossible to achieve. In order to communicate the desire of a manifestation, you need a clear picture, what your imagination wants to create.

Stimuli from your senses get captured in an organ in the brain that is sometimes referred to as the 3rd eye. The 3rd eye is present within the spirit and affects your entire body. It is not an actual eye. It does not necessarily reside in the head but many people think it is the pineal gland. This gland produces hormones and is the connecting organ for the 3rd eye. The 3rd eye is an extremely important component of your imagination. Without it, it would be difficult to picture the manifestation in your mind. The 3rd eye is therefore like the hard drive in a computer. In this hard drive many data can be collected and stored. The 3rd eye will sort and file its experiences systematically and without prejudice. The 3rd eye does not analyze any of the data it collects. The collected data will be analyzed by the superconscious. If some data is harmful, it can be buried under many layers; but if needed, this data can be retrieved.

If a person asks the superconscious to clear any injurious or harmful data, it will do so. For example, one who has suffered from a violent act such as incest or rape will only access the data when they desire too. If the act interferes with the spiritual development of the individual, it may be wise to void those memories. You would need to ask the superconscious to void out any specific memories and all energetic attachments associated with the event. It does not mean that the person will completely erase the memory, but it does mean that all the harmful emotions will be severed. Even though the memory banks may retain the factual evidence, there will no longer be a feeling about the event. A person may not experience sadness, anger, or other emotions and could choose to talk about it with no ill effect to the physical body.

Imagination may also be used as a clearinghouse, for if you can create it, you may also undo it. When your imagination is effective in clearing an event that occurred to the person, the memory of the event will vanish. Many extra-terrestrial visitors will direct their thoughts into the imagination of the person and thereby eliminate the memory of the visitation. If this is done properly, there will be no way to retrieve the visitation, even with hypnosis.

Your imagination is another way to help you telepathically communicate with the spirit world. There are no limits to the imagination. If you can think of it, it can be accomplished. Many of our technological inventions come from ideas that come from science fiction films. Remember, the soul records everything, including your ideas. When desire connects with imagination, then the result can be astounding. The Universe you live in really is shaped by your thoughts and our imagination.

Pineal Gland

When wanting to connect to the spirit world, you may feel you need to 'cleanse' your physical body. While it's important to keep a strong mind and heart, there's another, lesser-known organ critical to spiritual connection: the *pineal gland*. It is the pineal gland that receives visual messages from your soul.

This small gland, part of the endocrine system, is located right behind the pituitary gland in the middle of the head. The pineal gland makes hormones for sleeping, and it assists the pituitary gland and the hypothalamus. Its hormones consist of amino acids meant to aid the body with long-term organ regeneration. Therefore, the pineal gland has an indirect influence on life span.

The pineal gland looks like a small pinecone on the outside, usually about the size of a pea and no larger than a walnut. Yet on the inside of the pineal gland, there is genetic material that is like the rods and cones in your eye. It is for this reason that people have referred to it as the 3rd eye. For a long time, doctors didn't think that it served much of a purpose, but the spirit world tells us more. The spirit world says that without it, you do not have inner vision. In one sense, the pineal gland is your spiritual eye. When one astral travels, the things you experience are actually recorded by this 3rd eye. The pineal gland helps you perceive what your eyes cannot. A strong pineal gland leads to extended psychic abilities.

The pineal gland can be blocked from its functions by many things including poor lifestyle. This can include everything from eating a poor diet to not spending any time outside. The pineal gland can become weak and calcified, leading to less spiritual communication and lower levels of melatonin. Melatonin is a hormone produced solely in the pineal gland. It is important for sleeping, anti-aging, and protection from certain serious mental or physical ailments. It has a wide range of medicinal uses, such as for the potential treatment of Alzheimer's, cancer and diabetes. Fundamentally, it is an important tool for sleeping. The guides tell that in the absence of melatonin, it is difficult to be able to make a spiritual connection.

To connect with your spirit guides, it is important to decalcify your pineal gland. Even ancient civilizations knew that the pineal gland was important, so much so that they called it the "seat of the soul." More accurately, it could be called the seat of the spirit, as the soul resides outside the body. The pineal gland has been associated with seers and clairvoyants. If you want to be able to communicate better with the spirit world, you want your pineal gland to be healthy.

There are many ways to make your pineal gland stronger. The first way is to eat a healthy diet that does not include foods that are acidic. Stop using fluoride, chlorine, and bromide, for starters. Taking a bath or swimming in chlorine water is especially harmful to the human body and leads to a quick

Chapter 19 – Spirit Communication

calcification of the pineal gland. Refrain from drinking tap water, and keep away from pesticides, sugar, caffeine, alcohol and tainted tobacco.

Calcium supplements containing calcium carbonate can be harmful to your health. Calcium carbonate causes calcium build-up—not only in the pineal gland, but also in the arteries. If you must supplement your diet with calcium, choose natural foods like spinach, broccoli, sesame seeds and chia seeds. Your body can only absorb plant-based minerals. Minerals from rocks are not absorbable by the body, and deposits build up in your joints, circulatory system, and brain. If you are not getting enough minerals from vegetables, then use a plant-based minerals supplement.

Raw foods and foods that do not contain genetically modified properties are the best choice to consume. It is important to the overall health of your body as well, but to eat and drink unhealthy choices hurt the chances that you will be able to connect better to the spirit world. Berries such as blueberries and goji berries contain certain enzymes that the body needs to decalcify the pineal gland. Meat contains hormones that mess up the endocrine system and the body will send healing energy to other glands long before it sends healing to the pineal gland. You could hardly live without the use of your pineal gland. Raw chocolate, MSM, citric acid, garlic, raw apple cider vinegar, boron, and Zeolite are some of the better supplements for the decalcification of the pineal gland.

The second way to improve your pineal gland is to drink the purest water source you can find. Never drink tap water, even if used to make coffee or other drinks. For example, most gas stations produce coffee that comes from water straight from the city water systems. These water systems contain fluoride and chorine. Those things will ruin your chance to have a clear connection to the spirit world. Fluoride especially causes the pineal gland to develop calcium.

The third way is to go to bed when it gets dark out and awake when it is light. The pineal gland does not do well with artificial light, as you need darkness for the pineal gland to produce melatonin. Watching television or staying up late on a computer prevents the body from utilizing the pineal gland, and even those who are psychic become less psychic if they mess up their body's biorhythms. Sleeping at the right time will help you to become closer to the natural cycle that the body needs for healing. Fighting these natural cycles can lead to depression, and in some cases that can be devastating. Your pineal gland needs light during the day and darkness at night and when you change the normalcy of the cycle it can function improperly. In modern times, we normally do not want to go to sleep when the sun goes down. It helps to dim the lighting and stay away from screens before bed.

The fourth way is to develop the practice of sungazing when the Sun is setting or rising. It is dangerous to the retina to gaze at the Sun during most of the day. It is not something you would attempt to do if you don't understand the pitfalls of sungazing. It is important to do this practice carefully and consistently. You may start by gazing at the sunset for ten seconds at first and then increase this slowly by a couple of seconds per day. You must condition yourself slowly or damage to your vision can occur.

Note: *Never sungaze if you are impatient and are expecting immediate results.*

The Sun can activate your pineal gland. If you wear sunglasses as a practice you might be missing out on some of the benefits of the Sun. The more energy you get from the Sun, the healthier you will be but only to a point. The Sun can cause more damage than good if you abuse it. It is best to have thirty minutes in the Sun and usually not at the peak hours. Your entire body needs sunlight for at least fifteen minutes per day, and it is the same with your pineal gland.

There are nutritional supplements that you can use to help your body decalcify the pineal gland. Iodine is often short in the human diet, and the best way to absorb it is through your feet. You can rub in food-grade iodine on the bottoms of your feet. The iodine will absorb quickly without going through the absorption process. Another supplement that works wonders is fermented skate liver oil. Green Pasture from O'Neil, Nebraska, makes a fermented skate liver oil product called *Blue Ice*. The skate is a fish in the shark family.

It is also important that you are getting all the necessary fatty acids. The best supplement I have found is *Omega Magic*. It is emu oil capsules, which contain Omega 3, 6, 7 and 9, and these fatty acids contribute greatly to health. Omega Magic helps with the endocrine system, and in turn, the anterior lobe of the pituitary helps with the production of growth hormones, follicle-stimulating hormones, luteinizing hormones, prolactin, thyroid stimulating hormones, and a whole host of other hormones that aid the body with anti-aging and sexual potency. Omega magic can also help with the energy production in the cells because of its effect on the thyroid gland. Since it helps the body produce calcitonin, it aids in the decalcification of the pineal gland. Calcitonin is responsible for reducing the concentration of calcium in the blood.

Skate liver oil and emu oil both aid the pancreas, especially around the area known as the pancreatic islets, which produce hormones that are responsible for controlling blood sugar levels. Insulin acts to lower blood glucose, and the addition of these two compounds aids with the production of insulin.

Another way to decalcify the pineal gland is to start having fun in your life. Doings things that bring back the joy of your spirit will be a fast way to decalcify the pineal gland. Remember, your spirit uses your pineal gland as an eye into your world, so if you're enjoying your life, and giving your spirit healthy experiences, the pineal gland will become more activated.

However, don't forget that your spirit does not enjoy activities that break down the body. Things like alcohol, drugs, and smoking do nothing for the spirit. Things that are educational and informative such as inspiring lectures and seminars greatly enhance your spirit. Spending quality time with your family will also increase the spirit's joy of living. When the spirit is ignited, it flushes the body with light photons. The energy from these photons rejuvenates the physical body.

Hypnotism

Researchers use hypnotism to tap into the superconscious highway. They can inadvertently believe that they are tapping something in the subconscious mind. This is a common misunderstanding. When a hypnotist brings a patient into the deepest state of hypnosis, they are really tapping into the information at the soul—or the spirit world's level. This is attained by using the superconscious mind to connect to the collection of knowledge and understanding stored in the spirit world.

Hypnotherapy is not helpful if it only addresses the conscious mind. If the superconscious mind agrees, a therapist can access information that lies in the subconscious mind. It will not do so unless it feels that it will not be harmful.

For example, people use hypnotherapy to quit smoking. It works for some, but not for others. If the superconscious mind is convinced that the person's conscious mind wishes to quit smoking, it will allow the hypnotherapist to remove memories from the subconscious mind that caused the habit. In some cases, a person may be smoking as an agreement with their superconscious mind to avoid another bad habit such as overeating or depression. In these cases, it would not be in the best interest for hypnotherapy to erase the subconscious memory. In this example, a person can decide to change their contract with their superconscious mind.

However, it cannot do so with just one request. The request would have to be in the form of a prayer, and may have to be repeated many times. In this case, a contract can be changed, and the superconscious mind may allow the hypnotherapist to remove a previous conscious command.

When you ask questions to the subconscious mind it responds to your questions by attempting to unscramble a whole bunch of files. It doesn't mean to make things up but the answers can be utter garbage. This is a common misunderstanding, but the fact is that the subconscious mind does not have the best information. When a hypnotherapist brings a patient into the deepest state of hypnosis, they are really tapping into the information at the soul—or the spirit world's level. This is attained by using the superconscious mind to connect to the collection of knowledge and understanding stored in the spirit world. The information that is stored at the soul level is much more expansive and accurate. This is why it is so important that a hypnotherapist understands to access only the information contained at the soul level which can only be obtained by going through the superconscious highway.

Chapter 20 – Connecting with Your Guides

Since I was a young child, I had the ability to hear information about both the physical and the spiritual realms from my guides. For much of my life, I took for granted that people would know this same information; after all, it was given to me so freely from my guides. It wasn't until I met my current partner, Meg, who influenced me to read books concerning spirituality. It was then that I realized that much that is being taught is different from what my spirit guides had taught me.

At first, I had to question my spirit guides to make sure I understood them correctly. Had they given me accurate information? Sure enough, they had. Therefore, I began to ask questions about the materials I was reading. The spirit guides began making commentary as I read the information. I was surprised at how much of it was so far away from the truth. I realized that not too many people are hearing clearly from their guides.

I started to question other people to learn about their experiences in communicating with the spirit realm. I found that most people—if they could hear their guides at all—got very sketchy information and I could see how things could be so misconstrued. I likened it to a game of telephone, in that one person would hear a message and spread that message, but with each person putting in a slightly different twist. As these misunderstandings about the spiritual realm are distributed, they move further away from the truth.

Over my forty years of healing work, I have heard many people say they wish they could hear from their guides the same way I do. If we can understand some basic things about the Universe, such as how the conscious mind works, the three minds, the different realms, and the spirit and soul, you can develop a good working knowledge of what the Universe is. Then you can work on removing the doubt you have. You're taking the first step to hearing your guides better, simply by reading this book.

As you may have noticed, most everything on the topic of spirituality these days either contradicts itself or contradicts other printed information. This can confuse people and creates even more doubt. Even as you hear from your guides, you may not believe what you're hearing. Most people feel like they must be hit on the head to receive information from the spirit world. So, the more educated you become about what the spirit and soul is and how it interacts with the Universe, the easier it will be to make a spiritual connection.

As you learn more about the spiritual world, you can also begin to practice meditation to develop a connection with your spirit guides. However, know that this book is not an instruction manual on meditation. This is because I am not a professional expert on meditation myself. People have asked me if I meditate frequently. Many are shocked that my answer is no. You see, I have been hearing from my guides for so long, I have naturally reached that level of connection. Meditation is a good way to change the world. For techniques on meditation, I recommend reading books written by Sarah McClean of Sedona, Arizona. She is an authority on meditation and leads meditations at her business in Sedona if you ever have a chance to visit her. If not, her book is called, "Soul Centered" and published by Hay House. Also, quite useful in the Robert Monroe Hemi Sync technique that uses sound waves to alter brain waves. It involves listening to multi-layered sound through headphones or earbuds. The brain responds by creating a third sound known as a binaural beat that encourages specific brain wave activity. I have this this helpful for lowering blood pressure and getting you into the theta mind to fall asleep faster.

I believe that if you are having difficulty connecting with your guides, then meditation or hemi sync can bring you to a different state of consciousness and understanding that makes your connection clearer. I'm not an expert on meditation techniques. Again, feel free to research into techniques yourself if you want to further your connection to your spirit guides through meditation.

A simple technique to connect to your guides is to sit quietly with a pad of paper and write down any questions that you might have and listen for answers. It may help to write extensively on what you are thinking about to prompt the flow of information. The answers may come in subtlety while you are writing. You may not be able to distinguish them from your own thoughts. You may be surprised at the clarity of thinking your writing will reveal.

Another option in developing your connection is through music. Music is one of the most effective ways to alter your state of conscious perceptions, and thus to connect to your guides. It not only helps the direct connection to your guides, but also helps remove various distractions. I have found it useful in healing, for soothing the spirit, and for releasing tension. Many artists claim they feel high when they paint, draw, sculpt, and other creative endeavors. I have felt this same high from both listening to and performing music, and it is a feeling that is difficult to put into words.

Chapter 20 – Connecting with Your Guides

The better you connect to your spirit guides, the faster you feed your spirit. This is one of the most important things you can achieve from understanding this book. If you allow yourself a limited amount of time to connect to your spirit guides, then you can expect little success. But the more you work on this, the better it becomes. The personality must convince the superconscious mind that you really want what you ask for.

As a young boy, every night before going to sleep I recited the same prayer. This is the prayer I used: "Dear God, please lead me, guide me, and protect me from harm. God bless my mother, father, my brother, my sister, and my grandparents, amen." What I was asking my superconscious mind to do was to lead me and guide me, and eventually you do get what you ask for. What better way to lead you and guide you than to provide you a clear conscious connection with your spirit guides. This is the second time I have mentioned this prayer because it is so important to achieve your objectives.

Whether or not you believe your guides are listening is not important. Doubt does not sever the connection to your spirit guides. The spirit world understands that you are all going to suffer from fear, doubt, anxiety, and a variety of emotional disturbances. This is part of the reason you have guides. They help you navigate through this sea of confusion. Even if you believe that your guides are not talking to you, it is important to continue to talk to them. Thoughts go out into the Universe and do not suffer from interruption. They always hit their intended targets. You have been created with thinking capacities. If you are capable of thinking, you are able to connect to the spirit world. At times, you may get notions or ideas and you don't know where the ideas originated from. These ideas are telepathic transmissions from the spirit world. Sometimes these transmissions are just feelings; feelings with power and impact behind them. Even ideas you think are inconsequential might be transmissions from the spirit guides. Their intent is not to dictate your life, but to steer you on the right path. By putting slight notions into your consciousness, they are giving you clues that you can use on your mission. When you piece together all the clues in your life, you get a more comprehensive picture of what your objectives are. It is up to us to put together the puzzle. The guides are not there to do your work. They are there to steer you to the proper pathway to fulfill your soul's contract.

When a spirit volunteers to take the Earth tour, the spirit will sign up to play certain roles. Once the spirit incarnates it may not be able to remember what its roles are. Choosing the wrong roles could forfeit the spirits opportunity for spiritual growth. My guides call this loss of spiritual memory amnesia which is a risk that you take when you incarnate at this dimension. The guides are always ready to be of service. They will assist you in your mission in life by sending you warm, radiant love energy that has no limits.

Earth is one of the least-advanced societies in our Universe, but many high-level spirits have volunteered to come to Earth to assist in the conscious development. The spirits have a lot to teach to the less spiritually evolved beings and they knew it would not be easy. There is a risk of being trapped in the amnesia of the dense physical realm so that the spirit forgets the purpose for incarnating.

Guides communicate with you in a variety of ways. It would be difficult for God to directly connect to billions of people on Earth and can you imagine God having to communicate with the nearly infinite planets with life on them. That is why there are so many guides. God created them to be of assistance and it is not demonic like churches want you to believe. They might set signs or symbols directly in front of you as if to guide you. Others can hear an inner voice speaking to them, but it is not like an audible voice. Others have noticed that their lives seem to be orchestrated for them. The right people will show up in their lives to teach them the lessons that need to be taught at that moment. Guides are usually people who belong to your soul family and have a personal interest in you.

I am asked the question frequently, "How can I connect to my guides?" Although you are always connected to your guides, I usually discover that what people really want to know is, how they can hear from their spirit guides. Humans can use various methods to connect with the spiritual world. The easiest way is to ask the superconscious mind to connect you with your spirit guides. Don't ask for any entity to contact you but only the ones that are there for your highest benefit. Meditative states can be helpful to quiet your mind enough to hear your guides.

People who have had an out-of-body experience or have left the physical body as in a near-death or afterlife experience, can often connect with the spiritual world at will. I don't recommend you attempt a near-death experience to see what you discover. A lot do not get to come back so it is really suicide.

For the past three thousand years, religions have been demoting and diminishing the power of the spirit guides. The authorities of the ages went through a lot of trouble to make sure that all references to guides were deleted from the accepted teachings. The leaders of the times did not think that references to angels were any threat to the teachings but mentioning guides was frowned upon.

There are many references to angelic beings in the stories of the virgin birth and Jesus with his mysterious ascension into the clouds. These stories would not make any sense unless the events were attributed to the work of angels. Could Jesus have been lifted into a spacecraft? Was Mother Mary abducted by extra-terrestrial beings, and impregnated artificially? Modern technology has led rise to some critical thinking in this arena and the masses are just starting to put new meaning to the old stories.

People have entered into the spiritual realm or found themselves on what they believed was a spacecraft and have claimed to experience miraculous healings. Could this have occurred in the days of Jesus? It seems plausible. Many of these people believe they were endowed with abilities of advanced healing, psychic powers and unexplained pregnancies as in the time of Jesus.

You might find it difficult to grasp the concept that there are more advanced beings in the Universe than humans. Perhaps you cannot remember any past lives, or you have never had the feeling that you have lived in other dimensions. But more people are claiming that they believe there is more to life than we have been taught in schools. People fear what they don't understand. However, there are beings in all dimensions and beings that inhabit planets all over the galaxies. The ones that have visited Earth are commonly called "The Watchers." Sometimes these extra-terrestrial beings will act as chaperones to spirits. Some can become spirit guides.

Guides vs. Angels

Guides are extremely helpful if you allow them to be. Some people call guides angels, and I believe if you are communicating with angels, you are extremely blessed. So, what's the difference between them? It took me many years to make a distinction and I was amazed at how different they are. They are not even in the same realm! Here are the basics.

Angels are your best spiritual supporters, or your cosmic cheerleaders. No one has ever doubted that angels have your best intentions in mind, but many have doubted that angels even exist. That is partly since most people do not see angels in physical form. Other people report that they feel the presence of angels, but they do not see or hear them. If your intuition becomes strong enough, you can peer into other dimensions and see angels with your eyes.

Angels come from the angelic realm and guides come from the celestial realm. These realms exist side-by-side and are very different but complementary to each other. A realm is a more comprehensive term for a combination of dimensions. A dimension doesn't refer to the beings that exist there, just the place. According to the spirit world, a better term might be *density,* but we are so accustomed to the word dimension that it is used instead. We are not talking about dimensions as the way physics teachers do but today the word has not been invented that would better describe a place. We refer to ourselves as living in the 3rd-dimensional world, not the 3rd-density world. Because of this confusion, we will just stick with the term *dimension* even if it might not agree with quantum physics. In physics the word dimension refers to the measurement, rather than mass or volume. It represents the depth, height, length and breadth of an area. Density, on the other hand, refers to the mass per unit volume. So when I say dimensions in spirituality I am referring to a particular level of the Universe.

The celestial realm is not considered to be any greater than the angelic realm. They just appear to be equivalent to one another. Advanced beings can exist in either the angelic realm or the celestial realm, and there's no limit to who can visit either one. The angelic realm is named so because it is where angels reside, but they are not the only beings that reside there.

Guides and angels aren't completely different; both have no judgment on your life's decisions. I know this is not a difference that should need to be pointed out. However, the fact that you are doing one thing, and they are directing you to do something else could be seen as somewhat of a judgment. Though, they are not judging you but influencing you to get you back on the course that you incarnated for. It is not their opinion that you need to act like angels, such as how a parent might influence you. If you want to run around like a chicken with your head cut off, it will not embarrass guides or angels. They have no emotions of jealously, anger or fear, as we have. Angels are quite aware when you are getting into danger, so at that point they might become a little more obvious to you. They view every action in the most positive light and so in this sense they are your cheering section.

To work in the angelic realm, you must have a more hands-on approach to helping advance humanity. To qualify to work in the angelic realm, you had to have graduated as an advanced soul first. Most anyone could work in the celestial realm, and even become a guide for a time. All people have all been in all dimensions and for the most part unless you were a new soul once. New souls will have to first experience all thirteen dimensions before becoming a spiritual guide.

Chapter 20 – Connecting with Your Guides

Guides are with you daily to help keep you on your path. Guides are always there with you, watching over you. Angels, on the other hand, are summoned by your guides to help with emergencies. Life threatening situations are where you usually hear about angelic intervention. Although both angels and guides are energy-based beings, angels can also affect the physical realm. For example, a friend of mine had a motorcycle accident where he said he felt like he had fallen on a "bed of feathers". He walked away from a high-speed fall with not even a scrape or a bruise!

Angels are souls that have achieved liberation. They have developed enough self-worth that they have broken free of the reincarnation cycle. They may choose to reincarnate, but they don't have to. They are in a sense servant of the Universal Creator and messengers to man. The Hebrew and Greek words originally meant messengers.

Because angels reside in the Angelic Realm, few people can see them. However, angels do bleed through periodically into your dimension. You may only see them during a near-death experience. Angels are depicted with wings, but this is not always the case. They are beings of light that aren't necessarily in any form.

Angels help people when they cross over into the celestial realm. Many times, angels are guardians or guides that assist you in your daily life. Not all incarnates will have an angel as a guide, but those that do have probably been one.

Guides may be assigned to you by beings called the Enlightened Ones or Elders. Elders can stay in the celestial realm when they have completed many lifetimes successfully. These souls have satisfied their own requirements and mastered the lessons they set out to learn. The Elders teach people who enter the celestial realm, as well as help train guides.

Not all guides are strangers; your spirit may have agreed to have an old, trusted friend or celestial teachers to serve as your guides in this lifetime. Guides are souls who have lived many Earthly lives and have completed most of their Earthly education. There is also a review board to approve of their ability to work as a guide. Guides chose not to incarnate while they are guides but assist you from the celestial realm. Occasionally, they may send a little of themselves down to earth in the form of an animal to also help in that way. Have you ever heard the saying, "You don't choose your pets, they choose you."? Your guide may prod you to find the pet or sometimes the pet just shows up on your doorstep. Guides will not interfere in your life in ways that would have a negative impact. They mainly send hints and messages to help steer you toward the completion of your plans you chose to achieve in this life. You may notice that a recurring pattern appears in your life and the outcomes create greater and greater difficulties for you. Sometimes the guides must hit us over the head with the proverbial 'two by four' to get our attention. Once the pain becomes great enough you will have no other choice but to listen. Their hope is that you will finally look at what you need to achieve. Does this sound familiar?

Striving to be a Light Worker

When people are drawn to careers of teaching or the clergy, these people are rarely driven by money. These people are being motivated by their superconscious mind, to get into something that is in their spirit's best interests. They won't impress people and they won't likely make a lot of money. However, they may very well find themselves more fulfilled in life. This is because positions like these align with soul-nourishing functions. People like these can be called 'light workers'—they are interested in following their spirit, not their conscious mind. The term light worker is obviously a general term; the spirit's needs can vary between people, so a person is a light worker if they are following their specific spirit's needs.

Many light workers have been angels in the past. When I've done readings on people, I was surprised to find out how many incarnate angels are on Earth now. I remember reading information that angels are created by God, and that they never have lived a human life. I found this hard to comprehend, so I asked the guides if this was true. They said of course angels have been incarnated, hundreds of thousands of lives and are mostly older souls. A soul does not have to be incarnated as a human form. Most often, light workers have experienced life as a plant, animal, insect, and have completed the circle of life. That is, they have experienced life in dimensions in all realms. These are volunteers that have come back to help us during tumultuous times. It reminds me of a song that I once heard that reminds us that life is really love, and love is a battlefield. Light workers know that the job they have been assigned to is not necessarily going to be a cakewalk. However, these are advanced souls that have never been given more than they can handle.

Many light workers start out in the clergy or in the metaphysical fields. They tend to gravitate toward mystical information that will help to advance our civilization. Others tend to gravitate toward technology and environmental concerns. Most of them are not profit-motivated, but desire to aid and assist humanity. Quite a few of them understand that judgment is unproductive, and these people tend to have compassionate personalities.

Chapter 20 – Connecting with Your Guides

Many light workers work in healing professions, and some are even doctors. Light workers come from all "walks of life," because of the need to provide for themselves. When a light worker is trapped in a dead-end job, they become depressed, and are more likely to have physical ailments. If a person has a desire to become a light worker, they need to make a conscious connection to the spirit world.

Chapter 21 – Improving Your Intuition

Intuition comes to us from our soul, through our superconscious mind, in flashes. Intuition is defined as a direct perception of an inner truth that comes from the collective result of our own experiences. This knowledge called intuition comes from our souls and not from outside sources. It can be seen as a keen and quick insight, that feeling in the gut. It is distinct from psychic impressions, which we'll recognize as coming from the head. Psychic impressions arrive from entities outside of us; they come from other spirits or guides. Our intuitive knowledge, on the other hand, comes directly from the soul. It is important to understand that intuition can become stronger, and we can improve it directly.

Intuition often arises in situations where what we feel conflicts with the logic our mind is telling you. The mind may be telling us its right, but our gut tells us otherwise. Intuition may also arise in a dangerous situation. We might think you're going on a calm drive, but our intuition warns us to slow down, as there may be a deer on the road. Lo and behold, around the next corner we spot a deer. Intuition is our own souls seeing through what the personality or senses are missing.

We will now break intuitive senses into seven basic categories.

The Seven Intuitive Senses

Clairaudience is the perception of sound or communications from other dimensions. These sounds may be too low or too high in frequency to detect with the human ear. Some people report abilities to detect low frequency vibrations such as those put out by electromagnetic radiation, sunlight, and high energy particles called cosmic rays. Animals have an ability to hear sounds that could be other-dimensional.

Clairvoyance is the ability to see things that a normal person cannot. It enables the person to perceive scenes and mental images that cannot be perceived with the eyes. Clairvoyance can see things such as ghosts and beings of light that the average person cannot see. The proper amount of sunlight may improve the psychic senses and brief exposures to the sunset and sunrise may even increase the size of the pineal gland. The pineal gland is the gland that is most closely connected to the psychic realm. High level noises can detract from our psychic development and low level soothing sounds may improve it.

Clairempathy is the sensing of the emotions of another person. This person is most often referred to as an 'empath,' which is the same thing. Some empaths not only sense energy but take on emotions from others. There are many people who display an ability to understand the emotions of others just by reading their body language.

Psychometry is the sensing of an object's certain energies via touch or sight. These people will report that the object retains a memory and tells a story. People with this ability can gain information from an object by using their mind. This is largely a function of the superconscious mind that allows the person to connect and get information from an object.

Psychokinesis is the ability to move objects physically with thought. These abilities we are said to be born with, but we lose them over time and are rarely reported.

Psychic healing is the ability to cure pain or energy with the use of touch or mental projection.

Auric sight is the ability to perceive the field of energy that surrounds a physical form.

People ask me all the time for the difference between an 'intuitive' and a 'psychic.' How do we define the word psychic? Psychic differs from intuition in that it is a knowing and not a feeling. So a definition of psychic would be an inner knowing that comes from the spirit and is the result of the collection of our experiences. How would we define the word intuition? Intuition is an inner *feeling*.

Intuition also comes to us in our feelings about a situation. We can ask ourselves if something we are pondering would be good for us. When we ask, pay close attention to what emotions come up in the gut. If we feel a sense of constriction, an uneasiness, or fear or anger, our intuition is saying it is not for us. If we feel a sense of expansiveness, relief, or a positive feeling, our intuition is saying it is okay for us.

Our intuition shapes our emotional behavior. If we feel we are doing something that is wrong or hurtful, our emotional well-being will suffer. We can lie to our mind and say that we are not hurting ourselves or anyone else with our actions, but our physical body doesn't buy into the lie. It will give us signals if we pay attention.

Most of our negative thoughts have an injurious impact on our electrical system in the physical body. Negative thoughts can reduce the positive flow of electrons across cell walls and can cause damage to a particular organ. The human body has many backup systems that kick into play when there is an impediment in the flow of energy in the body.

Chapter 21 – Improving Your Intuition

Negative thoughts can be so powerful that they can even overpower all of the safeguards. Since we control all our thoughts, it is also entirely possible to affect each of our organs in a positive fashion so that they will not become diseased. When we use our intuitive senses, our feelings dramatically change. Perhaps we may even sense euphoria or a calming sensation coming over us.

The easiest way to improve our intuition is to act on our hunches and see how they directly improve the day. The more you see that our hunches are helpful, the more we will grow to trust our intuition and rely on it more often. It may be helpful to keep a journal of hunches or coincidences to help us recognize when our intuition has been in play. The more we begin to trust hunches, the more we will be able to discern whether it is an intuitive hunch or just our conscious thinking.

Our intuition is really our soul communicating to us through our feelings. Our environment can condition the body to ignore our feelings but only in extreme cases is it psychologically appropriate for us to block them. An example of a social environment that can cause us to disconnect from our feelings is if we are surrounded by a group of unruly alcoholics. This lack of feeling can shut down our intuition and cut us off from our soul's path. This social environment can become a huge distraction. Our intuition should be our guidance system and we should not allow distractions to become our guide. If your intuition suffers in any way from the distraction of the environment it can be difficult to get back on our intuitive pathway.

Any environment can become toxic to our intuition when it is no longer settling or calming to the mind. This can be the case if where we live or where we work is a toxic environment. We may consider a new job or a new home if the toxicity levels become too unhealthy. If a state is taxing us to the detriment of our business, perhaps we can move to a tax free state. What is important is that we act. Our intuition may tell us what to do, but we are the one that needs to respond to the feeling.

Things that distract our mind from creating positive interactions will impede our intuitive growth. The more distractions that can be removed, the more we can build up our intuition. We can either choose to deal with the distractions or we can choose to ignore them. To continue to allow distractions to affect us will not lead to any growth in our spiritual life.

Those people who have developed strong intuitive senses may begin to realize that they no longer fit into the chaos that the rest of the world lives in. There are always those people who were perhaps our friends for many years but they have a reluctance or inability to accept new ideas. These people that believe that reality never changes can ridicule those that have varying mental awareness.

Some of the smartest people who are redefining their old ideas can become separated from the social orders to which they once belonged. They may begin to seek out friendships with people who are not on destructive pathways. Although this might limit the playing field in a matter of speaking, it does not mean that the number of friends will decline. However, it might expand their circle of friends to a much larger geographical region.

The first step in improving our intuition is to remove the toxic distractions. Toxic distractions may have nothing to do with how polluted the air quality is, but it is certainly one possibility that should be considered. A toxic distraction can be anything from unwanted noise to a pain in the physical body. A healthy body will generate healthy thoughts. Our own negative opinions of ourselves can be a toxic distraction. The clothes that we are wearing can be toxic if they are uncomfortable.

The second step in improving our intuition is to be truthful to ourselves. We cannot be truthful to others if we are not truthful to ourselves. If we are trying to complete a project that we have no real interest in, it can be difficult to achieve the best results. If we are overworking our bodies doing things that we do not love but choose to do, we are not being truthful to ourselves. If we are involved in social activities that we know might not be in the best interest of ourselves then we are not being truthful to ourselves. If we are overeating because we enjoy the taste of food, we are quite likely having guilty feelings about the action. These guilty feelings are there because we are not being truthful to ourselves.

The third step in improving our intuitive senses is to limit our social circles to those that have similar energies. Our thoughts are vibrations. All vibrations have an impact in the Universe. Those people who have similar vibrations to each other are more likely to find interest in one another. People who have similar interests will develop friendships that invigorate our intuitive senses. These people become energetically connected to one another and think of each other at the same precise moment. It is important to understand that it is hard to bring friends up to our level of thinking. They have to be willing to meet us at our level with love and understanding.

The fourth step in improving our intuition is to develop our inner vision, of which our pineal glands are a part of. Not every advanced being will choose to use their inner vision, but it is something that all animals possess. Inner vision is very much a part of intuition. It is sufficient to say that each one of us can develop inner vision.

Chapter 21 – Improving Your Intuition

The fifth step in improving our intuition is to develop a clean way of thinking. The cleaner our thoughts become, the more we learn to accept that everyone has his or her place in the Universe. We can then achieve spiritual enlightenment at a much faster pace. Spiritual enlightenment is the final phase in mastering our intuitive skills.

Intuition is the precursor to communicating with other dimensional Universes. The realities within a dimension may be endless but the dimensions build slowly. There may be more than thirteen dimensions in the future but that could be millions of years from now. In any reality we choose, intuition is the master of it. It is one our key abilities. We choose the players, the components, and even the environment. It is our intuition that plays one of the biggest roles in this selection process.

A strong intuition leads us to greater imagination. There is no limit to our imaginational resources. Even resources that we once thought were useless can be helpful to the imaginative soul. The greatest ideas have not come from others but from within us and through intuition. It is difficult to extract any imaginative thoughts from those who are not willing to use their intuition.

Chapter 22 – Other Spiritual Beings

We may know someone who has encountered a ghost. We may even feel that we have seen an apparition. This is entirely possible; ghosts do exist, and they are spirits that are trapped in the Earth plane.

There are people that consider themselves Ghostbusters. They say that ghosts can only be released if you convince them to go to the 'light.' Although this may seem like a fairy tale, the spirit world tells me that Ghostbusters do have it right. The 'light' is something that all spirits see; it's a portal from the 4th dimension to the 6th dimension. We usually can't see ghosts because they are roaming around in the 4th dimension, alongside the 3rd. Only when someone is temporarily able to see into the 4th dimension do they see ghosts. Most times, how people experience the presence of a ghost is through non-visual ways, such as a menacing presence or cold feeling down the back of the spine.

If anyone had this experience, they, know that a ghost is usually unable to directly affect things in the physical realm. Certainly, many people have sworn that a ghost has pushed them or moved objects. A spirit can do small things, but only if it shifts part of its energy back into the 3rd dimension. It is rare for a spirit to achieve this, and for the most part, we should not fear them.

Although I have not encountered too many ghosts myself, I have been asked on several occasions to remove ghosts from a property. In all cases, this has worked quite well, but it is not because I have an ability to influence things in other dimensions. It was not me, but my spirit guides, who speak to the ghost-in-residence. In every case, my spirit guides informed the ghosts why they are not invited to stay in the residence. Sometimes, my spirit guides would tell the spirit to return to their soul.

The ghosts do respond to my spirit guides, who tell me why the spirits were sticking around in the first place. Sometimes, ghosts feel like there is some injustice that led to their death. Sometimes, they don't even know why they had to die. They may be afraid of ascending toward the white light and have not made contact with their guide or an angel that would help them cross. They may even be lingering because they want to stay by those they love. In a few cases, the loved ones left behind weren't allowing the spirit to leave, not accepting the others' death.

Surprisingly, there are differences in ghosts in the 3rd dimension and ghosts in the 4th dimension. Ghosts reside in the 4th dimension; they can see us when we are in our astral bodies, but they cannot affect our physical bodies. Ghosts can be a faint image in the 3rd dimension as they bleed into it, but they have no physical form.

Ghouls and Poltergeists

There are energies in the 4th dimension that feed off fear. They sometimes attach themselves to a physical body and can affect a person. These are not spirits; we call these entities ghouls. A ghoul is not a spirit from the Earth plane. It is an entity from another planet or star system. A ghoul has no power over you unless we let them. People who are in depressed states, mentally unbalanced, or who are experiencing addictions may attract ghouls, which only increases their problems. It is believed that drug addicts attract the most ghouls. People's actions while affected by ghouls are not the actions of their own spirit. Young children are also vulnerable to ghouls.

Poltergeists, on the other hand, are a being of another sort. They reside in the 4th dimension like ghouls, but rather than attaching to us and feeding off our fear, they *create* fear within us. They cannot affect our physical health but can affect our mental health. Like ghouls, they are from another planet, but they differ from ghouls in that they can affect all people, not just drug addicts, alcoholics, or depressed individuals.

Unfortunately, it is difficult to know if we have a ghoul. However, if we encounter a poltergeist, we will know it; there's no mistaking their unwarranted fear. Know that we can pick up ghouls by our own actions. Even hanging out with others who are addicted—like seedy bars, for example—may get us in contact with a ghoul. One technique of removing ghouls is to stare at a person who has a ghoul in the eyes. Ghouls do not like to be looked at. We could stare into a mirror if no one is around and we are concerned that we may have picked up a ghoul and demand that it leaves. If a child has a ghoul, we can look the child straight in the eyes and demand it leaves the child.

However, all is not lost, if we get either of these entities hanging around us. When we get rid of a personal addiction, we can remove a ghoul. We may also visit positive people such as healers, whose very energy and presence can send ghouls or poltergeists away. We may also ask your guides for protection, and they will keep entities away from us.

Even if we are just nervous about these entities, remember again that we can pray to the superconscious for protection.

Repeat to yourself every day this prayer:

"Dear God, please guide me and protect me."

Chapter 22 – Other Spiritual Beings

This was the beginning line of my childhood prayer. It worked quite well as I always stayed safe from these negative energies.

Chapter 23 – Short Answers to Controversial Questions

Was man made in God's image? No

Was man created from apes? No

Is the Universe round? Yes

Was Darwin's theory of evolution essentially correct? No

Does God exist? Yes

Do people reincarnate? Yes

Can Angels incarnate on Earth? Yes

Is there such a place as Hell? No

Has there ever been life on Mars? Yes

Does God favor one nation over another? No

Does God get angry? No

Does God hear each one of our prayers? No

Did the prophet Jesus Christ teach about the concept of sin? No

Does Satan exist? Yes

Is Satan the same as the Anti-Christ? No

Do animals have a spirit or a consciousness like a human being? Yes

Do plants have a spirit or a consciousness like a human being? Yes

Did Christ die on the cross to absolve our sins? No

Has there only been one Christ? No

Was the Earth seeded by extra-terrestrials? Yes

Are there extra-terrestrials living on Earth today? Yes

Were unicorns only mythical? No

Will there be a war to end all wars on Earth? Yes

Is life an illusion? No

Did the continent of Atlantis once exist on Earth? Yes

Is our planet advancing into another dimension anytime soon? No

Is the world coming to an end? No

Chapter 24 – A Review

First, let's review the key points in connecting to the spirit world.

Tell your superconscious mind that you would like to hear your spirit guides better than you currently do. Perhaps you have no understanding of how they are communicating with you at this time, and you want to establish the connection. Your superconscious mind will take care of getting the message to the subconscious mind. Your big responsibility is to tell your superconscious mind what it is that you want.

People want to ask their higher self and that really is commanding the superconscious mind. The higher self is an extremely small component of your superconscious mind. If you continue to think in terms of higher self, you are really limiting your chances of manifesting your desires. I have done one-on-one healings with many people who still think that they need to communicate with the higher self, and it really is of little use. Once you understand how the three minds really work, then you can go to the second step.

This step is where you acknowledge and utilize your thirty-one senses... Ask your superconscious mind to strengthen these senses and help you to understand how to use them. To make it easier, work on one sense at a time. It never hurts to keep asking the superconscious mind for this, because the subconscious mind loves repetition, and it works better if you continue to affirm what it is that you want.

Once you feel that you have understood the thirty-one senses, you can proceed to the third step. This step involves *healing your body*. One thing that you might find helpful is to understand that the physical body is designed to be active for at least forty-five minutes per day. It is important to do something physical for at least those forty-five minutes. The rest of the day is yours to do with as you choose. It takes time every day to care of your body. You do not need to connect with guides to have a happy life, but for those who wish to, it is important to start thinking differently. There is a lot of information in this book; much of it may be new information for you. It may take reading the book more than once to comprehend it fully. Even the second time through will be more powerful than the first. This is the way that you learn the most efficiently; three times through will give you the greatest understanding.

You have been taught many things that are really smokescreens to keep you from your true divinity. If you really believe that you need to give away your power to someone who is living or someone who has died, then you are really just falling for a smokescreen.

White light can protect you and draw you closer to angels. If you ask for the white light, know that this light contains all the colors of the spectrum.

The next most important thing you should do, whether you are interested in talking with angels or guides, is to take the time to *exercise your mind*. Then take the time to heal your mind. Your mind requires more maintenance than you might think. If you meditate five to ten minutes a day, it will go a long way in releasing things that are not meant to be there. You are not all the negative comments that you have heard, and you are not all the things that others may be projecting. You are love and you are light. You came to Earth to experience, feel connected with others and a variety of things. You also came here to create. If you have been doing a good job creating but you have not been experiencing, then your soul can become discouraged, and you will become depressed. If you are experiencing quite well but have not been creating, then it would be a good idea to start creating. If you quit creating, the soul thinks it is time to return to the source. You did come here so that you could return to the source, but with new experiences and new creations.

Some people know that they have a particular mission. Jesus came to express his divinity, to experience and to teach. He did an amazing job of teaching and when it was time, he returned to source. The one thing that Jesus did that was different from many men of his time was that he was in constant communication with his guides and angels that worked with him alongside any extra-terrestrial family. The virgin birth was a way of saying that Jesus was an implant into the Mother Mary from his extra-terrestrial parents. That confuses people, and I was a bit surprised myself to find that out.

While I was in the celestial realm during my near-death experience, I found out that Jesus does not channel to individual beings nor do angels. Jesus was a multidimensional being as well as a master teacher and his teachings continue to this day. There are people who think that they are channeling angels the guides knows that this is not true for the most part. There may be a few exceptions and a few gifted individuals may feel their communications do come from angels but according to my guides, it is extremely rare. I waited until the end of the book to drop this one on you. Why? It is because people get hurt quite easily when it comes to the topic of Jesus or angels. If you think you are communicating with Jesus or angels,

Chapter 24 – A Review

know that an aspect of you in your superconscious mind is the part that you are really talking to. That aspect is familiar with all the teachers in the celestial realm, and you can obtain many truths from communicating with your own self. Jesus explained that angels do not channel information directly to individuals unless they choose to incarnate. It is important to pay attention to angels, some of which are born into bodies but angels are giving us signs that they are with. Some angels will even share a body to communicate a point to someone who is not getting their messages any other way. But normally the person would not be aware that their message was even coming from angels. They would just be talking, and the words keep flowing like water. Again, they do not interfere or tell the person that they have been prompted to speak or give certain advice. They never tell you they are there.

If you find someone who is incarnated that has been an angel, then you are a lucky person. In my case, I have met a few because I tend to be a little stubborn and need a lot of redirecting.

Once we've done all these previous steps, then we are ready for the next step in communicating with guides. This is a lot to do first, and we should realize that it takes time to do all these things. If we get sidelined in any way by giving away our power to someone other than ourselves, then we will not be able to hear from our spirit guides. Hearing from our spirit guides requires that we reclaim our own power. We have to realize that we are a part of God and we are each important to God.

Reclaiming your power is difficult because we must first tell our superconscious mind that we want our power back. Most of us will never do that. I'm not sure why we become so reluctant to reclaim our power, but we would rather give away our power to those that have been brainwashing us for thousands of years. I'm not just talking about religion, but all the things that we are exposed to.

For instance, television commercials have done a superb job in convincing us that we need something. Chances are good we don't need what they are advertising, but we still buy their wares anyway. We live beyond our means, buying fancier homes than we need or cars we cannot afford. We are giving away our power to these institutions so that they can make more money. In turn we become consumed by debt; and focus on working harder to pay bills and collect more things, instead of creating, experiencing and returning to source.

During my near-death experience I was so shocked that Jesus does not want us to worship him. He did not come to Earth to start a religion that worships him. That too is giving away all your power. What he did teach is so different from what religions teach. I felt I had been lied to. Someone must have known that this was a lie. Jesus told me that we are all like him. I would like to be more like him and when I am making a tough decision, I sometimes follow the 'what would Jesus do' philosophy. This helps me but on other occasions, my guides must become really loud in order for me to understand what the best decision is.

We sometimes give our power away to our spouse. We want to do one thing, but they have a different idea. It is not wrong or right, but we are not getting closer to our soul's purpose if we always give in to our partner's desires. This must be a two-way street or there will be friction. Friction will not lead to a happier life, and it can cut us off from connecting with our guides. If you are ready to reclaim your power and not giving it away all the time, you are ready for the next step.

The next step is to get away from hostile environments. If someone wants to kill us, we should get away from them unless we really enjoy getting killed. If they are attempting to kill us the spirit should also get away. If you have an abusive spouse, we should leave and let them be. They have their own cross to bear and it is not fair for us to take it on.

Nothing kills our spirit more than doing things we hate all the time. If we are with people that are not inspiring and uplifting, then we need to choose better friends. Sometimes this might mean that we don't talk with siblings who are constantly bringing us down. Don't feel any guilt for this. Just remove them from our lives People have a lot of difficulty with this step and it is just a step. The longer you put it off, the longer it will plague us..

If one is reading this and you are part of a religion that makes you a little uncomfortable, leave. You don't owe these people anything. When I asked Jesus before I returned to earth what church I should join he answered, "None of them." So, I didn't, and it hasn't hurt me but became a way for me to reclaim my power.

If we can reclaim our power, then we can move forward to the next step. That is to *create*. If we are already creative, then continue to the next step. If we have a great deal of difficulty, then we really need to stop and ask ourselves what we really want to do with our lives. Perhaps at first it can just be something we do as a hobby or recreation in our spare time.

Most of us watch television in our spare time. That is what Americans seem to prefer. They want to be entertained and at the same time they want to bury their emotions. They do this with drugs, alcohol or by overeating. Instead of watching television, we could be creating. If we don't take the time to be creative, then the spirit does not see much of a purpose. A lot of this life is about nurturing our spiritual self.

The next step is to go out into the world and experience things. The reason we often don't is because of our financial issues, which is nothing more than an excuse. Seeing the world does not always require a lot of money. If we have not ventured very far away at this point, then just start by seeing what is in the state or region where we live. Chances are we will find things that we didn't even know existed. By joining social groups, we may make new friends that we enjoy.

One of the biggest reasons people don't seek new experiences is because of their fear of the unknown. These fears have been instilled into us by those who wish to control us or by our own insecurities. If we spend too much time embracing fear, there is no time to experience.

Now it is time to make our first attempt at channeling our own guide. Ask our superconscious mind to only bring in our assigned guide or guides to work with you. Do not worry that we will attract a low-level guide because there is no such thing. Teachers who have taught about channeling in the past have had the mistaken notion that there are low level guides and high-level guides. The spirit world wants us to know that they cannot be a guide unless they meet certain requirements. Guides only operate from a high level. If one thinks that they are communicating with a low-level guide, know that it is an entity of another sort. It is important to exercise caution when attempting to communicate with our guides.

If we get relaxed and focused before we connect with our guides, we will feel the confidence that a guide gives us. Ideas or notions may begin to pop into our head from out of nowhere. When these ideas seem quite foreign to our understandings, then we know that is from an outside source. When we feel good about the information, we know that it is coming from our guides and not some other low level being.

Guides do not normally tell us what to do. They give us suggestions in which we can choose to act on or not. If they do tell you, point blank, not to do something, then we should pay much closer attention. I have done things that my guides have said not to do, and it always turned out badly.

Do not attempt to make the first contact with guides when ill, grieving or in shock. If we are in times of crisis, it is better to wait until we are emotionally stable. Know what our true guide feels like. If a disembodied being comes in while we are in a lower vibrational state, it can really be confusing, and we might even be misled. Once we are connected to the spiritual world, we can talk to them when we are at a low point but it is not a good idea to attempt this in the beginning.

Channeling our guides is a skill and it can become refined over time. There are many channelers that will talk to any being that will talk to them. I only recommend talking to our own guides. Ask for this and be insistent. It would not be in the best interest to allow just any being to come in.

Each one of us has a head guide. He is called your father guide. He is the one that will gain our trust. Our guides will tell us things that confirm who they are. Other spirits will not be able to achieve confirmation. Our father guide knows us better than we know ourselves.

Okay, here is that seven-step process I promised everyone. Perhaps we will find our own way that works better, but here is my suggestion.

Find a comfortable position to sit in. Try to achieve the best posture you can, taking the pressure off your spine the best you can. I prefer sitting rather than lying down. If you get so used to lying down, you will not be able to channel too well for others unless you are lying down, and this may create a challenge if you are required to stand or sit.

Close your eyes and begin breathing slowly and deeply. Your breathing should be comfortable and in perfect rhythm.

Let out all your thoughts. Think of a mantra that makes you focus on nothing else in the room. This part is like meditating but you do not have to go into a deep trance. The reason why I don't suggest going into a trance is so that you can consciously channel and remember what it is that is being said. There are trance channelers that go in so deep that they do not remember a single thing that has been said. It is okay to do this but you will not benefit nearly as much if you do. Try not to fall asleep. Stay with the program. You are just trying to hear what your guides are telling you in this Universe… not some other Universe.

Mentally relax each part of your body, one by one, starting at your toes and continue up to your head. Do not think of chakras or any other smoke screen images that you have been taught in the past. No blue violet flames or reaching into your high self. Discard all the old notions that lead nowhere and think only about your guide.

You can put a bubble of white light around you for protection in the beginning, but later you will find out you can skip this step. Your guide will do the protecting once you have made repeated contact.

Once your body feels relaxed, you can start asking questions in your mind. Ask only things for things of the greatest intentions. Ask questions

Chapter 24 – A Review

that are spiritual in nature and let them know that you are ready to receive. Make sure you ask for things that are for your higher good.

Use a recorder to capture the information or write on a piece of paper. You can ask your guides if they would be so kind to keep the channel open while you are writing.

This step is the most important. Be quiet and listen. Many of us have this voice narrator that wants to talk all the time. The biggest problem the guides tell me in communicating with people is that they are asking questions, but they aren't hearing the answers. So, tune out the narrator. You can't hear two things accurately at once.

My hope is that this process is as automatic for you as it is for me. I can now turn it on like turning on a light switch, but I have been doing this for over forty years. If you did as much channeling as I have done, you may have a lot more books out than I have, but for most of my life I was not so willing to share this information. I was worried about what others may think, and of course, that is a normal human concern. As I got older, I became less concerned about what people think and more concerned about sharing the messages that I have been blessed with.

Conclusion

Now that you have some of the primary tools about the truth of your existence, what are you going to do with it? Will you share it with others? Will you begin a new journey, or will you make a transition in some area of your life? It is hard to continue leading the same life that you once led if you understand these truths.

I call you to action. When you successfully integrate this newfound understanding with your daily life, you really do get what you ask for. The Universe is truly at your beck and call. Stand for your truth and you will find love and positive energy.

I am going to give you a simple assignment. It is the easiest assignment you will ever get. I am asked all the time by people that I do readings for, "What is the key to happiness?" It is phrased sixteen-thousand ways, but the answer is always the same. The key to being happy is to *laugh*. Pretty simple, right? Find a reason to laugh every day. It releases chemicals called endorphins to the brain and bloodstream that makes us happy! The key to nourishing your spirit is to love something or someone: a person, a cat, a dog, a horse, anything.

I created an album to nourish the spirit that is jam-packed with messages of love called *Talking to the Choir*. It is a tool of higher learning. Surround yourself with tools of love and get rid of tools that destroy.

You might ask yourself, "What have I learned in this book?" What was the most exciting part? Was it learning of the superconscious mind? Was it the part about the circle of life? Each one of us are affected differently by different sections. Here is another huge surprise for you. I want to give you as a second assignment. Read this book three to six months, or even a year from now. You will find that the impact is different. Every year, every month, and even every day, you will gain new perspectives.

Now that you have taken your first step into hearing the truth directly from the spiritual world you might wonder how you can help. Please feel free to contact us at the David Armstrong Network by going to littleswanpublishing@gmail.com. To learn more and to keep updated on upcoming books click on the tab for upcoming events.

I congratulate you for reading this book. Your life will change for the better because the truth will always lead you toward the happiness and joy of the spirit. I wish you the greatest success in your journey and I am confident that you can change and improve your life.

It is time to awaken.

Made in the USA
Middletown, DE
09 December 2025

22265345R00119